HONOR
BEGINS AT HOME
THE **COURAGEOUS** BIBLE STUDY

Michael Catt • Stephen Kendrick • Alex Kendrick

Developed with Travis Agnew

Lifeway Press®
Nashville, Tennessee

AFFIRMFILMS **Lifeway**

Published by Lifeway Press®. © 2011 Sherwood Baptist Church
Sherwood Pictures, A Ministry of Sherwood Baptist Church, Albany, GA. All rights reserved.
Reprinted January 2018

ISBN: 978-1-0877-5678-3
Item: 005835997

Dewey decimal classification: 306.85
Subject headings: FAMILY LIFE \ DOMESTIC RELATIONS

Photography by Todd Stone
Publication design by Juicebox Design

To order additional copies of this resource: write Lifeway Church Resources Customer
Service; One Lifeway Plaza; Nashville, TN 37234; fax 615.251.5933; phone toll free
800.458.2772; email *orderentry@lifeway.com;* order online at *www.lifeway.com.*

Printed in the United States of America

Adult Ministry Publishing
Lifeway Christian Resources
One Lifeway Plaza
Nashville, TN 37234

CONTENTS

ABOUT THE AUTHORS

Michael Catt has served as Senior Pastor of Sherwood Baptist Church since 1989. The church has 3,000 members and has averaged one hundred baptisms each year. Thousands have joined the church from Albany and 29 surrounding communities, and the congregation has members from 20 different nations. The church has changed from a neighborhood church to a regional, multi-ethnic congregation with members from eleven nations. Sherwood has two campuses covering 100-plus acres—the main church campus and the upper school campus and sports park. The 82-acre sports complex, Legacy Park, is a ministry to the community with tennis courts, soccer fields, baseball fields, equestrian center, fishing pond, and large pavilion. "Path to Truth," the weekly broadcast of Sherwood's services, is available on the web and via podcast at www.sherwoodbaptist.net.

Michael and his wife Terri have been married since 1974. They are the proud parents of two grown daughters, Erin and Hayley.

Stephen Kendrick Stephen Kendrick has dedicated his life to serving Jesus Christ and to making Him known around the world. He is a co-writer for the screenplays and books and the producer for Kendrick Brothers' films.

Stephen has spoken to churches, conferences, and seminars around the nation, and has been interviewed by FOX and Friends, CNN, ABC World News Tonight, The Washington Post, and other media outlets. He is a co-founder and board member of the Fatherhood Commission. He graduated from Kennesaw State University and attended seminary before being ordained into ministry.

Stephen and his wife, Jill, live in Albany, Georgia, with their six children. They are active members of Sherwood Church in Albany.

Alex Kendrick is a follower of Jesus Christ and has a passion to tell stories of hope and redemption. He is a co-writer for the screenplays and books, and he's the director and editor for Kendrick Brothers' films.

Alex has spoken to churches, universities, conferences, and businesses all across America and in other countries. He has been featured on FOX News, CNN, ABC World News Tonight, CBS Evening News, Time Magazine, and many other media outlets. He is a graduate of Kennesaw State University and attended seminary before being ordained into ministry.

Alex and his wife, Christina, live in Albany, Georgia, with their six children. They are active members of Sherwood Church in Albany.

Travis Agnew worked with Sherwood authors to develop *Honor Begins at Home*. He serves as the Senior Pastor of Rocky Creek Baptist Church in Greenville, SC. Travis graduated from North Greenville University with a B.A. in Christian Studies and a Music minor. Earning his M.Div. and D.Min. from The Southern Baptist Theological Seminary, his doctoral focus was on family discipleship.

In addition to authoring Distinctive Discipleship, Wiki God, What God Has Joined Together, 5 Worship Team Killers, Don't Drop Your Kids Off at Church, It's All About God, and Freshman 15, he has also developed Lifeway curriculum with the Kendrick Brothers including the studies The Battle Plan for Prayer, Honor Begins at Home, The Love Dare for Parents, and The Resolution for Men Bible Study.

As time allows, he preaches at different conferences, events, and camps. He blogs frequently about faith and family here at travisagnew.org.

ACKNOWLEDGMENTS

From Stephen, Alex, and Michael:

We thank God for the many people who helped make *Honor Begins at Home: The COURAGEOUS Bible Study* a reality!

Sharon Roberts, for her kindness and diligence in overseeing this project;

Jon Rodda, for doing such a great job on the art direction;

Bill Craig, for his leadership and wisdom;

A special thanks to Dr. Thom Rainer and the Lifeway Leadership Team, who came to Albany in November 2009 and took seriously our request to spend a month in prayer about our partnership. It is obvious to us that the Lord has guided our steps in this process.

We are grateful to:

Travis Agnew, for his love of Scripture, passion for fatherhood, and diligence in fleshing out each session;

Jim McBride and Bill Reeves, for their friendship, representation, and marketing support;

Our loving wives, Jill, Christina, and Terri, for supporting us in ministry and in time away to work on this project;

Our fathers, Larry Kendrick and Grover Catt, for loving us, leading us, and modeling Honor at Home!

Travis wishes to thank:

Abba Father, for His perfect example of modeling true fatherhood to me;

Amanda, for being an even greater partner than I could have possibly imagined;

Obadiah and Eli, for giving grace to your father as he tries to follow God;

Our families, showing us Christ and giving us immeasurable love;

Phillip Howle, for your relentless accountability in my life;

Chuck Lawless, for supervising my doctoral project and passionately discipling me;

My discipleship group, for constantly pushing me closer to Christ; and

Pastor Jeff Lethco and North Side Baptist Church, for allowing me to share my passion for fathers with others.

ABOUT THE MOVIE

As law enforcement officers, Adam Mitchell, Nathan Hayes, and their partners in the Sheriff's Department, David Thomson and Shane Fuller, are confident and focused. They willingly stand up to the worst the streets have to offer. At a briefing, their sheriff highlights statistics illustrating the importance of a dad's involvement in kids' lives, and encourages them, "Go home and love your families."

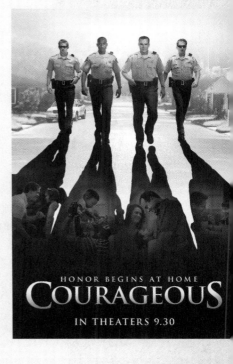

But what does that look like? While they consistently give their best on the job, good enough seems to be all they can muster as dads. Still, that's better than most men … or is it?

Challenged to search for answers about fathering, these men and their friend Javier discover a new sense of direction as they begin to understand that God desires to turn the hearts of fathers toward their children and the hearts of children toward their fathers (see Mal. 4:6).

As gang-related crime continues to plague their community, battles rage all around them. A new sense of commitment needs to take hold—both on the streets and in their homes. Will these men find a way to serve and protect those who are most dear to them?

Filled with action-packed police drama, *COURAGEOUS* is the fourth release of Sherwood Pictures, the movie-making ministry of Sherwood Baptist Church in Albany, Georgia. Filmed on locations in southwest Georgia, *COURAGEOUS* is Sherwood's first movie since *FIREPROOF*, the number 1 independent theatrical release of 2008 that has impacted millions of marriages in 75 countries.

As you begin this study, we challenge you to pray and expect God to do a fresh, transforming work in your family. We hope this study will help you more effectively go home and love your family with God's unchanging love!

INTRODUCTION
COURAGE TO BE HERE

Welcome! Fasten your seat belt and get ready for a challenging adventure in God's Word. The key themes of the movie *COURAGEOUS* are also the focus of this Bible study. During the next eight weeks, you will learn about embracing your identity in Christ, walking in integrity, winning and blessing your children's hearts, and much more. You do not need to have attended the movie to participate in this study—but you definitely will want to see it!

Fully utilize this book in your small-group session as you take notes, answer questions, mark Scriptures, and make commitments. You may be participating in a church campaign or attending a men's study in the workplace. However you're involved, plan to participate fully.

Bring your Bible and invite a friend to join you. *COURAGEOUS* creates interest and conversations you might not have otherwise. Pray for God to work in amazing ways in your group and in other small groups.

The movie's law-enforcement motif permeates *Honor Begins at Home.* Each session includes the following elements:

GROUP EXPERIENCE

BRIEFING	***Instructions***
	Session briefing helps the group enjoy being together, learn what the session is about, and move into the topic.
STAKEOUT	***Clips from COURAGEOUS/Interactive Bible study***
	Authors Stephen and Alex Kendrick set up clips for discussion. Group interacts with God's Word.
10-4 MEN/WOMEN	***Application***
	In police settings, 10-4 means *acknowledgement received* and acted on. Depending on your group, men and women might do application separately.
TAKE THE WHEEL	***Commitment/Prayer Time***
DURING THE WEEK	Read assigned chapters from *The Resolution for Men* and *The Resolution for Women.*

All video clips for this Bible study are available for free at lifeway.com/courageous. Optional readings in this book add detail to a topic raised during the session. For more information on and the availability of *The Resolution for Men* (Stephen and Alex Kendrick with Randy Alcorn) and *The Resolution for Women* (Priscilla Shirer), see *www.lifeway.com/courageous*.

There's something for everyone in this study, though this is clearly a study about biblical fatherhood. If you are a man, are married, and have children, you no doubt are concerned about the challenges that face families today. Some days you wonder what to do next in your own family.

We commend those of you who are single, who have come because you want to better understand and prepare for being a spouse and parent in the days ahead. You may be married, with no children yet, and want to form a godly foundation now with your wife. You may have children but no spouse, and you desire to better understand and succeed in your role as a single mom or dad.

You and your spouse may be attending together; your efforts toward godly parenting are strengthened as you walk this journey together. If you are a mom, you have a direct hand in bringing up sons who will one day be fathers or bringing up daughters who will one day choose a man to marry who will serve as father to her children. You may be a grandparent wanting to maximize your influence in this season of your life.

Regardless of your circumstance, we challenge you to take courage and let God use this study to help you leave a strong legacy for many generations! It takes courage to take the first step.

GROUP VALUES

As your group begins this study and meets together for each session, it is vital that together you commit and agree to group values similar to the ones listed below. Once these values are agreed upon, your group will be on its way to experiencing Christian community.

PRIORITY: While we are in this study, we will give high priority to group meetings and to the commitments we need to make to our families.

PARTICIPATION: Everyone is encouraged to participate. No one person should dominate.

RESPECT: Everyone is given the right to his or her own opinion, and all questions are encouraged and respected. Spouses respect each other in how they respond in the group.

CONFIDENTIALITY: Members will be prompted to share thoughts and feelings related to the family they were raised in as well as the family they are forging now. These expressions are made in trust and should be kept in the strictest confidence. Anything private shared in the session should remain there.

LIFE CHANGE: The goal of the small-group experience is transformation. Each session will help us identify aspects that need attention in our walk and relationship with Christ.

CARE AND SUPPORT: Permission is given to call upon each other at any time, especially in times of crisis. The group will provide care for every member.

ACCOUNTABILITY: We agree to let the members of the group hold us accountable to the commitments we make in whatever loving ways we decide upon. As a group, we choose to commit together to the accountability that is necessary to stay the course and live a courageous life.

_____

SIGNED

_____

DATE

ACCEPTING
YOUR
RESPONSIBILITY

THE MAN GOD IS CALLING YOU TO BE IS THE
MAN YOUR CHILDREN NEED TO FOLLOW.

"As for me and my house, we will serve the LORD."
JOSHUA 24:15, NASB

BRIEFING
GETTING THE RUNDOWN FOR THE DAY

GETTING TO KNOW EACH OTHER

Perhaps you're a busy parent who wants more for your family. You've followed the *COURAGEOUS* movie and are curious. Maybe you resonate with the unapologetic call for men to live courageously for their faith and their families. You fear for all that confronts kids today.

Whatever background and experience you bring to this group, welcome. It takes courage to be here, but it will be worth it.

Welcome! Introduce yourself to your group with the following questions.

1. Imagine that your family is about to move into a new home. Before you can occupy it, what steps must be taken?

To purchase and move into a new home, you must attend to a number of details—home inspections, contracts, financial agreements, and more. Moving consumes your time and energy.

If your family were to craft a family motto or crest for your new home, what would it look like?

An emblem, motto, or declaration can reveal a lot about focus and priorities, remind family members what they value together, and reveal to others what is important to your family.

While certain things are necessary for a family to occupy a home, have you ever thought about what is required for a child to *leave* that home? What do our children need to possess by the time they leave the nest? What kind of people should they be? How are we as parents making sure they have all that they need to thrive once they are living beyond our care?

Unfortunately, more time is often spent preparing to occupy a house than turning it into a home. Making a house a godly home starts with recognizing and accepting our God-given roles and responsibilities. It means recognizing that our children are a gift from God.

2. How do you think the majority of dads and moms would define "successful parenting"? How would you answer?

In research to address this question, 1,200 respondents measured success when children were characterized by:

Having good values (25 percent)

Being happy adults (25 percent)

Finding success in life (22 percent)

Being a good person (19 percent)

Graduating from college (17 percent)

Living independently (15 percent)

Being godly or having faith in God (9 percent)[1]

Families are taking their cue from culture, with disastrous results. Only 14 percent of the parents surveyed indicated they were familiar with what God's Word teaches about parenting, and only 9 percent view their parenting through the lens of faith. You may be here attuned to Scripture's teachings or be clueless about God's thoughts concerning parenting. Either way, you'll learn with other people who are walking the same path as we see courage raised up through God's Word and through the story line in *COURAGEOUS.*

Regardless of where you are today, the eight-week journey on which you are about to embark can change your life. You will be challenged to get out of your comfort zone, work through hidden issues from your past, and make strategic sacrifices for the sake of your family and your faith.

Are you up to the challenge of raising that 9 percent statistic related to rearing children of faith? It all starts with you and your relationship with your Heavenly Father.

STAKEOUT

INTENSE CONCENTRATION ON THE SUBJECT

A TIME TO STAKE OUR FAMILY ON GOD'S WORD.

COURAGEOUS CLIP

Watch *COURAGEOUS* clip 1, "Not Good Enough." Discuss using question 3.

→ **All video clips are available for free at lifeway.com/courageous**

3. **Why was "good enough" not good enough for Adam? How did his
friends react?**

A FATHER'S CHOICE

For Adam Mitchell, raising the bar meant intentionally accepting the
stewardship God had given him to mold the lives of his children. He knew
this would not be easy, so he called on a few of his trusted friends to keep
him accountable.

Later in the movie, Adam's resolve to be a better dad would ultimately
express itself in the bold affirmation, "As for me and my house, we will

serve the Lord." To understand the weight of such a resolution, let's put it in context from the Old Testament Book of Joshua.

When the great leader Moses died, Joshua took the reigns of leadership of God's people. God charged Joshua to be strong and very courageous (see Josh. 1:6-7,9), and Joshua obeyed. His commitment to risk everything for God would, for years, help Israel to win battles and allow Israel to take back what rightfully belonged to them.

Fast-forward to chapters 23 and 24. The war for the land was over, but the war for the family was just beginning. Before the people entered their new land and life, Joshua removed his general's hat and put on his pastor's hat, so to speak. He circled Israel around and gave the people one final challenge before this new phase of their lives.

4. Read Joshua 24:14-24 and write any key phrases that stand out to you. Circle one or two that impact you.

What did Joshua want to happen practically that day among families?

Joshua urged the people to choose to follow and obey God alone. That choice meant getting rid of other gods they had accumulated on their journey (vv. 15,19-20,23). Note how the people were witnesses to one another of their decision to worship and obey God (vv. 22,24).

Joshua knew he wouldn't be leading the masses much longer but resolved not to let the masses deter his family. While the culture would go in all directions, as for him and his family, they would stay faithful to the Lord.

5. What factors from the past make it hard for you to lead your family spiritually like Joshua?

You can take a bold step by taking a first step. It may be spending an extra hour a week with your family. If you're not where you want to be, this group can help you blaze a new trail of faithfulness.

15

A FATHER'S CHARGE

Someone must stand up and set the direction for a home. In Ephesians 6, the apostle Paul clearly set the standard.

Read Ephesians 6:1-4.

Paul exhorts children to obey and honor their parents. By honoring their fathers and mothers, children will be blessed with the promises of God. While parents rejoice at the message of these verses (and its possible applications!), Paul makes another distinction.

6. **In some form or fashion, parents are mentioned three times in these four verses. Write the specific words used to describe them in the order they are mentioned.**

1.
2.
3.

Children are called to obey and honor both father and mother, but here Paul singled out fathers with the task of spiritual instruction. The apostle had been using the word *mother* in his writing until verse 4.

If you are a woman reading this verse, don't be defensive. It has less to do with your role and more to do with raising the standard for the man who is to gladly assume his responsibilities. In many homes, mothers are the primary disciplers of the children, and that is exactly why Paul singled out fathers. Since the garden of Eden (Gen. 3:6,12,17), too many men have stood by passively when they should lead in standing for holiness in their homes alongside their wives.

7. **What did Paul command fathers to do and not to do (see Eph. 6:4)? Practically, what would each of these things look like in your home?**

8. What would happen to the next generation of children if fathers around the world took seriously this one command in their homes?

COURAGEOUS CLIP

Watch *COURAGEOUS* clip 2, "Adam's Speech," and listen for phrases he used to challenge men to lead in their homes.

➔ **All video clips are available for free at lifeway.com/courageous**

9. How does Adam's speech illustrate his desire to live out Ephesians 6:4? How will you respond to his challenge?

"BE ALERT, STAND FIRM IN THE FAITH, ACT LIKE
A MAN, BE STRONG." 1 CORINTHIANS 16:13

10-4 MEN
HEARING AND ANSWERING THE CALL

A TIME TO APPLY WHAT WE'RE LEARNING

If your group is coed, you might considering moving into separate men's and women's groups now for a time of personal and family application.

If your coed group remains together during this time, use the "10-4 Men" section for your application activities.

SELF-EVALUATION

10. **If you were to consider your parenting up to this point, what are you getting right as a husband and father? Be specific.**

How do you see yourself falling short? Be specific.

What in this lesson challenges you as a father?

THE PERFECT EXAMPLE

Accepting the responsibility that God requires of us as fathers can feel overwhelming. One of the main problems is that many men haven't seen what a courageous father even looks like. We need look no further than our Heavenly Father.

Read Ephesians 3:14-19.

In verses 14-15, Paul reveals God as the perfect Father. We don't call God *Father* because He is like us earthly fathers; rather, we are called *fathers* because we need to be like Him! While your earthly father may disappoint you at times, your Heavenly Father is the perfect example you need. He is the Father we all need, and He is the Father we all desire to be like.

11. Circle the character traits you think God as Father possesses.

Disconnected   Understanding   Careless   Strong

Negligent   Respectable   Honest   Breaks Promises

Patient   Loving   Weak   Easily Angered   Intimate

Passive   Provides   Actively Involved

All earthly fathers are flawed and a long way from being like God. Yet, when a child looks at his earthly father, he should be able to see qualities of our Heavenly Father: a loving Provider, a strong Protector, a truthful Leader, a respectable Authority, an excellent Example, and an intimate Friend.

If God is able to do far beyond what we ask or think—as He is—what do you hope He will do in your home during the next eight weeks?

10-4 WOMEN
HEARING AND ANSWERING THE CALL

A TIME TO APPLY WHAT WE'RE LEARNING

If your group is coed, you might considering moving into separate men's and women's groups now for a time of personal and family application.

SELF-EVALUATION

10. **If you were to consider your parenting up to this point, what are you getting right as a wife and mother? Be specific.**

How do you see yourself falling short? Be specific.

What challenges you in this lesson as you begin to discover what God requires of fathers?

THE PERFECT EXAMPLE

Accepting the responsibility that God requires of us may feel overwhelming at times. One of the main problems is that many of us haven't seen what a courageous man and father looks like. We need look no further than our Heavenly Father.

Read Ephesians 3:14-19.

In verses 14-15, Paul reveals God as the perfect Father. Earthly fathers don't call God *Father* because He is like them; rather, dads are called *fathers* because they need to be like Him! While your earthly father may disappoint you at times, your Heavenly Father is the perfect example. He is the Father we all need, and He is the Father earthly fathers desire to be like.

11. **Circle the character traits you think God as Father possesses.**

Disconnected   Understanding   Careless   Strong

Negligent   Respectable   Honest   Breaks Promises

Patient   Loving   Weak   Easily Angered   Intimate

Passive   Provides   Actively Involved

All earthly fathers are flawed and a long way from being like God. Yet, when a child looks at his earthly father, he should be able to see qualities of our Heavenly Father: a loving Provider, a strong Protector, a truthful Leader, a respectable Authority, an excellent Example, and an intimate Friend.

If God is able to do far beyond what we ask or think—as He is—what do you hope He will do in your home during the next eight weeks?

TAKE THE WHEEL

RETAKING LEADERSHIP WITH YOUR FAMILY

A TIME TO MAKE PERSONAL AND FAMILY COMMITMENTS

Holding onto the steering wheel is an iconic word picture in *COURAGEOUS,* starting with the first scene. The movie challenges men to take hold of the wheel, to hang on tightly, and to never fall asleep at the wheel. God calls men to take the lead in their homes and to fight for their families.

This personal journaling section allows you to begin to set in place some important personal and family commitments. Activities can be done at the end of each session in your group or you can do them on your own.

Write adjectives to describe your Heavenly Father.

Father, You are ...

To which two adjectives do you need to give extra attention in your own life?

I want to be like my Father in these areas:

Write the names of your family members below. Complete this thought. *God, I have a long way to go. I ask for Your help to reflect Your character and to be the man or woman of God that this person needs me to be.*

FAMILY MEMBER

ATTRIBUTE OF GOD AS FATHER YOU WANT TO BETTER REFLECT

Father, by Your grace, I will courageously accept the responsibility You have given to me. Now help me take the next steps.

COMMIT TO MEMORY

"As for me and my house, we will serve the LORD."
JOSHUA 24:15, NASB

A PRAYER FOR COURAGE

Dear Heavenly Dad,

I am amazed by the great love You have shown me. You love me so much that You are willing to call me a child of Yours. God Almighty, who knows everything about me, chooses to love me as His child.

You have provided for me, but I have turned away so many times. The lures of other gods take me out of focus in devotion to You. I am sorry when I take my eyes off You, even more so now because I know my shortcomings affect those I love the most.

My family needs a man of God. They need me to joyously accept the responsibility You have given me. I will not conform to the patterns of this world. I cannot force any other family to follow You; but as for me and my house, we will serve the Lord.

Amen.

COURAGEOUS HOMEWORK

For men only—In *The Resolution for Men*, read:
- ☐ "Why We Need Men of Resolution" (pp. 11–23)
- ☐ "Resolve to Be a Man of Responsibility" (pp. 55–69)

For women only—In *The Resolution for Women*, read:
- ☐ "The Resolution Revolution" (pp. 1–7.)
- ☐ "The Secret" (pp. 17–22)
- ☐ "Purposely Feminine" (pp. 31–48)

Option for parents to read together:
- ☐ "Final Speech from *COURAGEOUS*"
   (Appendix 9 in *The Resolution for Men*, pp. 248–50)

OPTIONAL READING

WHAT COMES TO YOUR MIND WHEN YOU THINK ABOUT GOD?

Some people do not like to hear a certain word used. It is bothersome to some and downright offensive to others. Due to the past so many people have experienced, to call God *Father* is the worst possible name to ascribe to Him. It leaves many Christians unsure how to view God.

Let's face it: we live in a fatherless world. Deadbeat dads are a cancer in our society. A majority of children are growing up in homes with fathers either physically or emotionally estranged from them. So when a person with baggage from his earthly father enters into discussions about the Heavenly Father, it's easy to see why he or she may struggle.

Pastor and theologian A. W. Tozer stated, "What comes into our minds when we think about God is the most important thing about us."[2] The implication of that thought cannot be overstated. Your perception of God has everything to do with how you live for Him. The problem is many people view their Heavenly Father in the same way that they view their earthly father.

If their father was absent, they may believe God is not concerned with their lives. If their father was too strict, they expect God to be a strict unforgiving judge. If their father was a passive disciplinarian, they often engage in sinful areas since they have always gotten off the hook before.

We have reversed the order. Many think we call God *Father* since He is like our fathers. In reality, we call our dads *father* because they are to be like God.

The apostle Paul said, "For this reason I kneel before the Father from whom every family in heaven and on earth is named" (Eph. 3:14-15). God creates and even names all family members. Fathers get their name from Him, not vice versa.

So if your earthly father was less than desirable in your life, don't make God pay for it! God is not trying to be like your dad who has fallen short. God is a perfect father (see Isa. 9:6) who gives good gifts to His children (see Matt. 7:11; Jas. 1:17). As a father, He carries us (see Deut. 1:31), molds us (see Isa. 64:8), and lavishes us with love (see 1 John 3:1). He dwells with those who lack an earthly father (see Ps. 68:5).

Whatever your situation, you do not or did not have a perfect earthly father. Don't make God pay for his mistakes. Realize that what you didn't have in him, you have abundantly in our Abba Father (see Gal. 4:6).

EMBRACING YOUR IDENTITY

YOU CAN'T GET RIGHT WITH THEM
UNTIL YOU GET RIGHT WITH HIM.

"Look at how great a love the Father has given us
that we should be called God's children."

1 JOHN 3:1

THE WEEK IN REVIEW

How's your resolve? Tools to help you are the *Resolution* books for men and women. They provide additional Scripture, motivation, and examples of courageous parenting to think about during the week.

How did this week's reading inspire you to take a stand for godly manhood or womanhood?

Name one of the seven principles Stephen and Alex Kendrick use to define manhood (p. 67). Which one was a new thought for you?

1. Who mows the lawn at your house? Takes out the trash?

Men are wired to accept responsibility. Embracing responsibility is part of manhood, and God wants to empower us to lead our families. We must get busy cultivating and protecting everything within our jurisdiction.

As we view clips from *COURAGEOUS,* our appreciation grows for all it takes to serve in law enforcement.

2. Would you make a good law enforcement officer? Why or why not?

The pressure on these public servants is extremely demanding. Imagine that you are an officer deployed on a special mission. You have just been informed of the whereabouts of one of the deadliest gangs in your state.

Your sergeant sends you to arrest these gang members without giving you a partner, backup, weapons, or protective gear. In addition, someone tipped off the gang about your impending arrival, and gang members know you are the one who put their former leader behind bars.

How good are your chances at success?

Your chances for success are about as good as succeeding as a courageous father without the Spirit of God empowering you. The task of being a courageous father is even more daunting than the mission mentioned above. In John 15:5, Jesus stated, "I am the vine; you are the branches. The one who remains in Me and I in him produces much fruit, because you can do nothing without Me." For many dads, their results have nothing to do with their intention and everything to do with their redemption.

3. **Write your answer here, but don't share it with anyone:**
   On a scale of 1 to 10 *(1* representing *deadbeat dad* and *10*
   representing *Super Dad),* how would you rate yourself in your
   fathering over the past year?

   Why did you give yourself this rating?

You may spend the next 10 years trying to move up a couple of numbers, but unless you have experienced a saving relationship with Jesus Christ and have His Holy Spirit guiding you, then your efforts will be in vain. Your family is at stake, and you can't get right with them until you get right with Him.

The path to heaven is not built by consensus. It has not and will never be put to a popularity vote. Someone gets to heaven only by the way that the Maker of heaven provides. It would be a disservice not to stop and state the obvious: It is impossible to be all that God wants you to be on your own. You need Someone to step in and do the work of grace for you.

STAKEOUT
INTENSE CONCENTRATION ON THE SUBJECT

THE GRACE OF GOD

In the Book of Ephesians, the apostle Paul vividly describes the power and grace that comes from what Jesus Christ accomplished when He died on the cross. The first two highlight the incredible blessings God gives those who place their faith in Christ. In order to help people understand and experience those blessings, Paul gave a lesson in explaining grace.

Read Ephesians 2:8-10.

4. **What phrases did Paul use to describe salvation in Ephesians 2:8-9?**

In verses 8-9, Paul states that good works cannot save us. However, in verse 10, he says we are to have good works.

How do you reconcile these two statements?

We are not saved by good works, but good works will show up after we are saved. If good works don't save us, how is someone saved? We are saved by faith, which gives us a new identity and perspective in Christ. Salvation is an undeserved free gift of grace to demonstrate God's kindness toward us.

5. **Complete the boldface words on page 31 to build the acrostic GRACE. Each word is included somewhere in the description.**

GRACE

G _____

Everyone and everything has been created by the one and only holy *God*. He has ultimate say regarding how people are to live their lives.

R _____

Sin is *rebellion* against God, and everyone has chosen to walk away from Him.

A _____

All people rebel against holy God. God sent His only Son, Jesus, to take the punishment for our sins. He offers forgiveness and righteousness to us through Jesus' death on the cross and resurrection. You may hear the word *atonement* used to describe this sacrifice.

C _____

When someone believes and accepts the gospel message, repents of his or her sin, and places trust in Christ for salvation, that person is saved. You may also hear this described as *conversion*, or being born again.

E _____

God's grace transforms anyone who repents of sin and trusts Christ for salvation. God promises believers *eternal life* with Him in heaven for all eternity, and He gives us a new quality of life now.[1]

Salvation is a free gift of grace that God offers to anyone who is willing to turn from their sins and trust in Him.

COURAGEOUS CLIP

In the introduction to the video, listen carefully to the background Stephen Kendrick sets about Nathan and David. Watch *COURAGEOUS* clip 3, "Gospel at Gun Range," and debrief with your group.

→ **All video clips are available for free at lifeway.com/courageous**

6. What impressed you with Nathan's gospel presentation?

God was convicting David about his past failures as a dad and his need for Him, and Nathan listened and responded sensitively. Nathan did not stop to make a formal presentation but shared his faith with someone he knew and cared about. He and David were friends as well as coworkers.

Rather than judging David, Nathan highlighted God's justice and holiness. He shared what had happened to him—he was a new man in Christ—and how a person can be saved. Correcting a common misunderstanding of salvation by good works, Nathan gave David an example he could understand. Asking whether David understood what he had shared, Nathan called for a decision.

Nathan was living out his faith and sharing it with others. He was ready. He also was learning a lot about what it means to be a courageous dad.

7. As you watched this clip, did you think of friends or acquaintances who might need to know the gospel? How could you share that message with them as Nathan did?

8. What do you also learn from this clip about taking responsibility as a parent?

YOUR TESTIMONY

While people may resort to arguments concerning Christianity, no one can argue with true results and personal experience. The best witnessing technique is to share your testimony, or your own faith story.

Paul shared his testimony three different times in the Book of Acts (see chaps. 22; 24; 26). In each occasion, he shared three key elements: (1) his life before Christ, (2) his conversion experience, and (3) his life after Christ, how he had changed. Read part of Paul's story in Acts 26:1-23.

9. What do you notice about Paul's testimony?

To better grasp our own conversion and improve our abilities to share our testimony, we need to practice. If we can't be courageous in this group of friends, we definitely won't be when the opportunity presents itself.

10. Write key phrases that describe your story in these three areas:

B.C.   **CONVERSION**   **A.C.**

(BEFORE CHRIST)   (AFTER CHRIST)

With a partner, share your testimony in the same amount of time (or less) as it might have taken Paul in Acts 26:1-23. If you don't have a testimony of salvation, then be honest with your partner about this and ask for his or her help in obtaining one.

So many people secretly doubt whether they truly know Christ and will go to heaven when they die. This is too important for us to not be absolutely sure. If you are not confident in your salvation, then use today's lesson for assurance, "Test yourselves to see if you are in the faith. Examine yourselves" (2 Cor. 13:5). Let today be the day that you truly turn from your sins and cry out to God for forgiveness of your sins and for His free gift of eternal life.

If you are a believer, then take time to stand amazed at the power of the gospel and commit to sharpen your skills in sharing His message with others who need to know Him personally.

> "GOD, WHO IS RICH IN MERCY, BECAUSE OF HIS
> GREAT LOVE THAT HE HAD FOR US, MADE US ALIVE
> WITH THE MESSIAH EVEN THOUGH WE WERE DEAD
> IN TRESPASSES. YOU ARE SAVED BY GRACE!"
> EPHESIANS 2:4-5

ABIDING DAILY

In some final words to His disciples before He was crucified, Jesus taught them what it means to abide in Him.

> "REMAIN IN ME, AND I IN YOU. JUST AS A BRANCH
> IS UNABLE TO PRODUCE FRUIT BY ITSELF UNLESS IT
> REMAINS ON THE VINE, SO NEITHER CAN YOU UNLESS
> YOU REMAIN IN ME. I AM THE VINE; YOU ARE THE
> BRANCHES. THE ONE WHO REMAINS IN ME AND I IN
> HIM PRODUCES MUCH FRUIT, BECAUSE YOU CAN DO
> NOTHING WITHOUT ME." JOHN 15:4-5

Abiding in Christ means staying in close fellowship with Him. We do this daily by praying to Him, confessing our sins, seeking Him in His Word, and walking in love and obedience. We must be constantly connected to Christ in order to succeed at anything. Apart from the Source of our salvation and our life, we are unable to do anything. With Him and in His power, all things are possible.

If your group is coed, you might consider moving into separate men's and women's groups now for a time of personal and family application.

THE GRACE OF GOD

11. **How would you describe the grace of God to someone?**

What part of it don't you understand completely, if any?

YOUR TESTIMONY

12. **How are you claiming your identity in Christ and leading your family to do so?**

13. **What part of your faith story do your children not know? What part can you begin to share? (See p. 42, "The Second Greatest Story.")**

10-4 WOMEN
HEARING AND ANSWERING THE CALL

THE GRACE OF GOD

11. How would you describe the grace of God to someone?

What part of it don't you understand completely, if any?

YOUR TESTIMONY

12. How are you claiming your identity in Christ and abiding in Him?

13. Do you and your husband share a story of faith as a couple? If you've not articulated it yet, how could you work on that together?

This personal journaling section allows you to begin to set in place some important personal and family commitments. Activities can be done at the end of each session in your group or you can do them on your own.

To embrace your identity, you must first be changed by the grace of God.

In order to solidify your salvation experience and give you assurance, how would you answer if Jesus asked you "What gives you the right to enter heaven?"

What does it mean to be a child of God? (See 1 John 3:1 on p. 39.)

Who in your life needs to hear how Jesus changed you by His grace? Think about those in your home, office, neighborhood, or church. How will you be ready to share this week?

COMMIT TO MEMORY

"Look at how great a love the Father has given
us that we should be called God's children."
1 JOHN 3:1

A PRAYER FOR COURAGE

Dear Gracious Jesus,

Your grace still amazes me. You are the holy God who demands my allegiance, and yet I have rebelled against You time after time. Unwilling to leave me in my state, You came and took my rightful place on the cross and provided atonement for my sins.

I have heard this message of love and forgiveness, and I am asking that Your Spirit bring my dead heart back to life. I turn from my rebellious ways and trust You in faith for my salvation.

Not only did You defeat death, but death has lost its power due to Your resurrection, and I can live with You for eternity. Let me forever marvel at Your grace and continually share it with those who need Your good news. Thank You for changing my life forever.

Amen.

COURAGEOUS HOMEWORK

The Resolution for Men, read:
- ☐ "A Lifelong Vision of Fatherhood" (pp. 25–37)
- ☐ "Resolve to Lead Your Family" (pp. 71–85)

The Resolution for Women, read:
- ☐ "Divine Appointments" (pp. 68–74)
- ☐ "I'd Like a Word with You" (pp. 79–85)

OPTIONAL READING

HOW TO ABIDE IN CHRIST

Many cars come with OnStar® capabilities. When in trouble, the driver can push a button and help comes. Once the crisis is averted, the driver dismisses OnStar helpers and goes on the rest of the journey.

A number of parents approach life the same way. When crisis comes, they hit their knees and beg for divine intervention. Once God helps them out of the situation, they see little use for Him anymore. Actually, if we think we can make it one step without God, we don't comprehend the Person with whom we are dealing.

Jesus also told them, "If you remain in Me and My words remain in you, ask whatever you want and it will be done for you" (John 15:7). Here, Jesus revealed our need for prayer and Scripture in order to abide. To remain in Christ means to have a constant connection with Him.

Our relationship with Him is more than spending a few rushed minutes in the morning. Instead, we are to pray (talk to and hear from God) without ceasing (see 1 Thess. 5:17).

Abiding also means allowing the Bible, God's Word, to go deep and come alive in us. More than gaining biblical knowledge, we also make personal application (see Jas. 1:22). Abiding means allowing God's Word to completely change how we think and act (see Rom. 12:2). One who *associates* with Jesus Christ reads His words sporadically, but one who *abides* in Him knows His words so they are near for guidance all day long (see Ps. 119:9-11).

By relying on prayer and the Word, you will find yourself constantly going to Christ for His strength and His answers to your situations. Ask God now to help you to abide in Him every day.

THE SECOND GREATEST STORY
YOU WILL EVER TELL YOUR CHILDREN

Many of you became a Christian before your children were around. Even if you became a Christian later in life, your personal testimony is not information they inherently receive. The greatest story you will ever tell your children is God's story of how He brought redemption to mankind. The second greatest story is how your story intersected with God's—the story of your salvation (see 1 Thess. 2:8).

As your children grow, they will have different levels of belief concerning faith. Depending on their ages, you will use different wordings or will select different portions of your story to tell. But you cannot begin too early to share with your children how Christ makes all things new in your life.

In Psalm 78:4-8, the psalmist provides an excellent framework for sharing your testimony with your children. He addresses the need to speak of (1) the faithfulness of God, (2) the frailties of the current generation, and (3) the potential of the next generation. These verses teach that if parents can share their personal shortcomings, then perhaps their children could bypass similar mistakes.

In sharing your testimony with your children, don't give all the details. Your kids don't need to hear you recount every mistake of your past, but it is beneficial for them to hear that you struggle just as they do and that Jesus makes all the difference.

When Paul shared his testimony in Acts 26, he provided a great example to follow. He shared what happened *before* (see vv. 4-11), *during* (see vv. 12-18), and *after* (see vv. 19-23) Jesus saved him. This outline is a great way to start constructing your testimony to share with your children.

1. What were you like *before* Christ? (Pray concerning how much to share.)
2. What happened *during* conversion? (When? Where? Why? How?)
3. What has your life been like *after* that moment? (How has Christ continually changed you?)

As you tell and retell your story to your children, you will be amazed at how they will view the most pivotal person in their life—you (even if you don't feel like it sometimes). *Your* story will play a significant role in *their* story.

REDEEMING
YOUR HISTORY

IF YOU WANT TO CHANGE YOUR FUTURE,
YOU MUST FIRST REDEEM YOUR PAST.

"If possible, so far as it depends on
you, be at peace with all men."
ROMANS 12:18, NASB

Often our journey toward becoming courageous is hindered more by past events we have never gotten over than by current obstacles. Our past becomes baggage that holds us back.

1. **Share the normal packing procedures for your family vacations.**

Who does what?

How does packing cause silly tension in your home?

Has someone ever packed so much for a trip that the baggage became a hindrance? Briefly describe what happened.

Perhaps your attempts to become all that God has called you to be seem sluggish at times. What slows us down? Maybe the problem is not what you desire to accomplish, but what has already transpired. We all have regrettable moments in our past—some we have caused and others that have happened to us. We cannot overlook them any longer.

2. **If you could go back and change one thing in your past (something you have done or something done to you), what would you change?**

THE WEEK IN REVIEW

In Christ, a believer's identity is brand new. Based on your readings during the past week:

How is your personal daily walk with God changing your family?

What opportunities is God placing in your path to share His love and forgiveness with others?

What ideas did you discover this week that you plan to try with your own children?

Strong relationships don't happen because people never hurt each other. They happen because the people involved keep on forgiving, empowered by the love only God can give.

Last week we focused on receiving the forgiveness of Jesus for salvation and following Him with our lives. Appropriately, now we concentrate on how His forgiveness changes us. We will be going to the back of the car to do a very difficult but very courageous thing: unpack the baggage that is slowing us down. We will be looking at our responsibility when it comes to:

(1) Offering forgiveness to those who have hurt us; and

(2) Requesting forgiveness from those we have hurt.

Before we can move forward, we must redeem our history. Only the courageous will proceed.

45

STAKEOUT
INTENSE CONCENTRATION ON THE SUBJECT

OFFERING FORGIVENESS

Think about what it means to offer forgiveness as you read Matthew 18:21-35.

Peter's willingness to forgive his brother seven times was not nearly enough, though listeners at the time perceived that number to be radical. The Pharisees, religious men of the day, thought that to forgive someone three times was the maximum required. Jesus answered Peter's question by setting a higher standard and offering a vivid word picture of the nature of true forgiveness.

Jesus often taught in parables. In this one He compared two debtors. The first man owed his master 10,000 talents. (One talent was roughly the equivalent of 20 years' wages for a common laborer.) In modern times, if a worker earned $15 an hour, he would make approximately $30,000 in one year. According to one commentary, a talent's equivalent in our economy would roughly equal $600,000, making this man's debt to his master insurmountable (about $6 billion).[1] In a shocking move, the master "had compassion" (v. 27) and forgave him of all his debt.

The second slave owed this newly forgiven servant 100 denarii. (For perspective, a common laborer in Jesus' day earned about one denarius a day.) While not as much as the first debt, this amount was still a substantial sum of money—equal to 20 weeks' work, or approximately $12,000 today.[2] Even after being forgiven of a multibillion-dollar debt, the first servant was unwilling to forgive a fellow servant's debt of $12,000.

3. What parts of this parable remind you of times people have hurt you?

COURAGEOUS CLIP

Keep in mind Michael Catt's experience as you watch clip 4, "Nathan at Grave." Discuss the clip as a group using activity 4.

➔ All video clips are available for free at lifeway.com/courageous

4. Based on what you heard in this scene, what justifiable reasons did Nathan have to hate his father?

How do you think Nathan's unwillingness to forgive his father might impact other relationships?

Has your father (or another family member) ever hurt you in such a way as to leave a huge "unpaid debt" in your life? Just acknowledging this hurt privately can be important.

Too many people have been deeply wounded or abandoned by their fathers. In fact, more than 24 million American children—about one of every three— live without the presence of their biological fathers.[3]

Most of us have legitimate reasons to not want to forgive people who have hurt us. Whether our fathers were good dads or bad, we all have likely been wronged or hurt by them at some time. Jesus teaches that these wrongs must be forgiven. In a sense, each of us has someone who probably owes us at least $12,000. That's a real debt that hurts. It has significant impact.

What reason did Nathan give in this clip for finally being able to forgive his father?

We cannot forget how much God has forgiven us—the equivalent of an impossible-to-pay-back $6 billion debt. The cross changes everything. Christ has every reason not to forgive us; yet, He offers freely the forgiveness that cost Him so much. His forgiveness changes how we act, feel, and think. Just as we have been forgiven so much, we must also forgive others (see Col. 3:13). We are to forgive without keeping count (see Matt. 18:22).

Read Romans 12:17-21.

Intentionally seeking peace and not allowing anger and hurt to build frees us to forgive others, release the baggage of past hurts, and move on into the future. It refreshes us spiritually, physically, and emotionally. Intentionally begin now to practice taking this higher way. You can break the patterns of past hurt and behavior even if no one else does. Do it for your children.

Read Matthew 18:33-35 again.

As Nathan's actions in COURAGEOUS illustrate, you can pray and fully release your imperfect earthly father from any and all the deep hurts he may have caused you in the past. You can do that now.

Is there anyone who has wounded you whom you have not fully forgiven? Is God the Judge or are you? Isn't it time to turn all of your hurts over to Him, the only righteous and perfect Judge? Take a moment now and pray to fully forgive anyone who has hurt you in the past—in the same way Christ has fully forgiven you.

REQUESTING FORGIVENESS

In addition to forgiving those in your past for the mistakes they have made, it is equally vital to request forgiveness from others for the mistakes you have made. Both actions require courage.

Read 2 Corinthians 7:10.

In this verse, the apostle Paul explains two types of grief: godly grief and worldly grief.

5. How do you distinguish between these two types of grief?

GODLY GRIEF   VS.   WORLDLY GRIEF

Worldly grief is what we feel when we are sorry we got caught and grieve over the consequences we face. Godly grief is when we are sorry we transgressed against holy God and hurt Him and others. Just feeling bad about past mistakes is not enough. Guilt doesn't accomplish anything; it merely exposes sin and urges us to action.

If you possess the kind of remorse that characterizes godly grief, you will want to repent (turn around), confess to others how you have wronged them, and take responsibility for your mistakes. Although Jesus has paid our spiritual debts before God in heaven, we are called to take responsibility for reconciling with those we wrong on earth. We cannot go back and undo the past, but we can do our best now to bring healing and restoration. Then, and only then, can we move forward. Remorse that leads to repentance can bring about new patterns of living for your entire family.

"IF YOU ARE OFFERING YOUR GIFT ON THE ALTAR, AND THERE YOU REMEMBER THAT YOUR BROTHER HAS SOMETHING AGAINST YOU, LEAVE YOUR GIFT THERE IN FRONT OF THE ALTAR. FIRST GO AND BE RECONCILED WITH YOUR BROTHER, AND THEN COME AND OFFER YOUR GIFT." MATTHEW 5:23-24

According to Matthew 5:23-24, Jesus puts the responsibility in our hands to reach out to those whom we have wounded in the past and to seek their forgiveness. His requirement is this: Before you engage in worship, find whomever you might have hurt and do your best to make amends. Then, our past mistakes become a powerful witness of the wonderful things God has done in our lives, as we demonstrate our willingness to humble ourselves and demonstrate God's love and care for those we have wronged.

Write the names of some people who may have something against you for which you need to reconcile.

Regardless of what has happened in the past, God wants you to take responsibility for what you have done.

COURAGEOUS CLIP

Watch *Courageous* clip 5, "David's Letter," and discuss using question 6.

➔ **All video clips are available for free at lifeway.com/courageous**

6. **How did David "start where he was" to take full responsibility for his past mistakes?**

Once David decided to send that letter, what possible outcomes did he have to anticipate?

Based on situations you know about, how do many people tend to respond to past mistakes?

David was different now because he had come to know God through a personal relationship with Jesus. That relationship made a difference in how he viewed his family, his past, and his future.

He admitted he had hurt Amanda deeply and that he had a daughter who might still need and want to know him. David honored God by asking Amanda for forgiveness and possible restoration. What he once viewed as a mistake was actually a gift and an opportunity God had given him. David faced his fears to do what was right.

God's grace gives us the strength and the desire to go back and make things right with others. We see this in the life of Zacchaeus after he experienced salvation in Jesus.

"ZACCHAEUS STOOD THERE AND SAID TO THE LORD, 'LOOK, I'LL GIVE HALF OF MY POSSESSIONS TO THE POOR, LORD! AND IF I HAVE EXTORTED ANYTHING FROM ANYONE, I'LL PAY BACK FOUR TIMES AS MUCH!' 'TODAY SALVATION HAS COME TO THIS HOUSE,' JESUS TOLD HIM, 'BECAUSE HE TOO IS A SON OF ABRAHAM. FOR THE SON OF MAN HAS COME TO SEEK AND TO SAVE THE LOST.' " LUKE 19:8-10

A desire to make amends grew out David's own gratitude for God's forgiveness. The Holy Spirit and supportive friends helped him start the process of reconciliation. By beginning to let go of his past and its destructive patterns, David helped establish a better scenario for future generations. His actions were helping Amanda and Olivia get off the road of pain and loss and onto a path of peace and restoration.

God calls each of us to lay down our pride, face our fears, and take responsibility for our past. We too have the Holy Spirit and other believers to support us in this courageous journey.

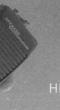

If your group is coed, you might consider moving into separate men's and women's groups now for a time of personal and family application.

OFFERING FORGIVENESS

7. Do you ever experience feelings of regret, anger, or disgust toward your father? For what?

How has your father's role in your life shaped you as a father (for good or bad)?

Your life story with your father makes a difference in how you parent your own children.

Is there anyone in your past, including your dad, whom you sense the Holy Spirit leading you to forgive right now? How can this group help and encourage you?

REQUESTING FORGIVENESS

Generally, a child greatly respects a parent who is willing to admit and apologize for past mistakes.

8. **Who in your home deserves a heartfelt apology from you?**

What would be the risk of offering this apology?

What's holding you back? Remember, leaders don't wait on others to get their act together first; leaders take the first step.

9. **What courageous steps will you take this week to humbly request forgiveness from those you have wronged? How can this group encourage you and help hold you accountable?**

10. **How do you think letting go of your past might impact your parenting and your family?**

OFFERING FORGIVENESS

7. Do you ever experience feelings of regret, anger, or disgust toward your father? For what?

How has your father's role in your life shaped your expectations for the other men in your life (for good or bad)?

Is there anyone in your past, including your dad, whom you sense the Holy Spirit leading you to forgive right now? How can this group help and encourage you?

REQUESTING FORGIVENESS

Generally, a child greatly respects a parent who is willing to admit and apologize for past mistakes.

8. **Who in your home deserves a heartfelt apology from you?**

If someone asked your husband what you thought about his success as the man of the house, how do you think he would answer?

Is there anything for which you need to request your husband's forgiveness in order to help him succeed?

9. **What courageous steps will you take this week to humbly request forgiveness from those you have wronged? How can this group encourage you and help hold you accountable?**

10. **How do you think letting go of your past might impact your parenting and your family?**

This personal journaling section allows you to begin to set in place some important personal and family commitments. Activities can be done at the end of each session in your group or you can do them on your own.

In the area of offering forgiveness, what specific steps will you take this week?

ACTION	TARGET DATE

In the area of requesting forgiveness, what specific steps will you take this week? Look back at the list you started on page 55 or 57.

ACTION	TARGET DATE

COMMIT TO MEMORY

> "If possible, so far as it depends on you, be at peace with all men."
> ROMANS 12:18, NASB

A PRAYER FOR COURAGE

Dear Father God,

Thank You, Lord, for the sacrifice of Your Son. Through Him, You have shown me mercy and, as the psalmist writes, removed my sins as far as the east is from the west. You no longer judge me as condemned.

I have been wronged. Though the pain I feel is real, I'm asking You to set me free from the chains of any bitterness from my past. Though it is hard, I know that the right thing to do is to forgive my dad and others from my heart. Today, by Your grace, I am choosing to honor You as the true Judge of persons who have hurt me in the past.

Therefore, right now, I choose to fully forgive and release

_____ from the pain caused me. I turn that pain completely over to You.

Father, I have also hurt others. Grant me a humble spirit to take responsibility for my mistakes and request forgiveness from those I have wronged. Let them see this change in me and give You the glory for it. Prepare their hearts to forgive me. And help me take courageous steps now to make things right with them as best as I can.

Amen.

COURAGEOUS HOMEWORK

The Resolution for Men, read:
- ☐ "Resolve to Reconcile with Your Past" (pp. 169–81)
- ☐ "Resolve to Live with Integrity" (pp. 183–95)

The Resolution for Women, read:
- ☐ "Overflowing Blessing" (pp. 23–27)
- ☐ "My Forgiveness" (pp. 127–43)

OPTIONAL READING

UNPACKING THE U-HAUL
The Problem with Emotional Hoarders

A cable TV show has exposed us to people who are unable to part with their belongings. These hoarders hold on to everything to such an extent that they become unaware of how their stuff is suffocating their lives. When they decide to move to another home, hoarders finally begin to comprehend how much baggage has been weighing them down.

We do the same things emotionally. We try to move along in our lives, but we have stuff in the back of the U-Haul® that slows down the process. Sometimes these bags are heavy. Sometimes we let a lot of small, light ones fill up the space we have. Some items are well hidden or are beneath another box.

Just like hoarders, you have some baggage you have collected and some baggage you have received. Both need to be addressed.

The biblical character Joseph lived with all types of baggage. As the favored son of Jacob, his prideful stories told to his brothers kept him out of favor with everyone in his family except his father. His brothers beat him and sold him into slavery. While taking a stance for purity, he was wrongfully accused of rape. After helping others out while in jail, he was left and forgotten to rot in prison.

Joseph had baggage. Some he collected, some he received; but he had to deal with both.

Joseph's handling of his baggage provides us an excellent example to follow. When he was in a position to retaliate, he chose to forgive. Speaking to his brothers who had beaten him and sold him into slavery, Joseph affirmed, "You intended to harm me, but God intended it for good to accomplish what is now being done, the saving of many lives" (Gen. 50:20, NIV).

Joseph knew that the past was past. Even while people had hurt him, that fact could not be changed; but he was wise enough to know that God alone had the power to bring good out of that evil. The apostle Paul reminds us that we too can "know that all things work together for the good of those who love God: those who are called according to His purpose" (Rom. 8:28). No matter whether mistakes have been made by you or to you, God is able to bring about good.

Collected Baggage. Concerning the baggage you have collected—those mistakes you have made—it's time to clean up the mess. If you have hurt others in the past, you need to address the situation. Realizing that God can make good out of your mistakes, go forward, praying for reconciliation and redeeming the work to be done.

Received Baggage. Concerning the baggage that others have dropped off, you still need to clean up the mess. Forgiving those people in the past will allow you to truly love all people today. Don't make current relationships pay for the mistakes of people in your past.

No matter who did the evil to you or to someone else, we serve a God who makes all things good.

SESSION 4

WALKING
IN INTEGRITY

A MAN OF INTEGRITY REFLECTS GOD
AND IS ANSWERABLE TO HIM.

"Why do you call Me 'Lord, Lord,'
and don't do the things I say?"
LUKE 6:46

BRIEFING
GETTING THE RUNDOWN FOR THE DAY

We all have that one yearbook photo we wish had never been taken. Most of us are thankful that Facebook® wasn't around when we were growing up.

1. What is your most embarrassing, humorous, or regrettable fashion phase, hairdo, or hobby?

We can each think back to a moment we wish we had done something differently. We each regret a phase, a date, or an activity that is forever linked to our past.

2. What do you see your children doing now that might embarrass them in years to come?

Don't you hope to spare your children the mistakes you made?

In 1987, the Partnership for a Drug-Free America launched an antinarcotics campaign with a series of public service announcements. Out of that initiative, one commercial became a social-iconic phrase. The short commercial highlighted a frustrated father confronting his teenage son after finding drugs and drug paraphernalia.

Upon being questioned about how he learned to use drugs, the son angrily shouts back, "You, alright! I learned it by watching you!"[1]

Our families do not need us to say one thing and do another. They long for courageous integrity. If we expect our children to learn godliness when they see inconsistency in the home, we are kidding ourselves.

We cannot drop our kids off at church and bring them home to a pathetic example of Christianity. We must walk with integrity and start that walk in the home.

THE WEEK IN REVIEW

As a review of last week's readings:

What are possible outcomes of the bitterness and guilt that accompany unforgiveness?

(Women) Priscilla shared the analogy of a retired circus pony to describe the cycle of unforgiveness (p. 137, *The Resolution for Women*). Indicate whether you think this description is effective.

Agree or disagree: "If you see a man of impeccable integrity in his old age, you can be sure he made his character a priority over the years" (p. 193, *The Resolution for Men*). Share reasons for your answer.

STAKEOUT
INTENSE CONCENTRATION ON THE SUBJECT

A STRONG FOUNDATION

As Jesus taught crowds of people, He knew that many were hearing His teaching but not applying it. They were hearers of the Word but not doers (see Jas. 1:22).

Read Luke 6:46-49.

3. **What do these two houses have in common? What differs? List what you see.**

House 1 (vv. 47-48)	House 2 (v. 49)

Storms raged against both houses. One man dug deep, building his home on a foundation of rock, and the fierce waters never did shake it. In contrast, the other house was built on the ground, without any foundation at all; when the torrents came, the building collapsed immediately. Not only did it collapse but its destruction was great.

Both builders had heard the word of God, but only the one who obeyed it survived and flourished.

COURAGEOUS CLIP

Watch Courageous clip 6, "The Two Tests," and debrief as a group.

→ **All video clips are available for free at lifeway.com/courageous**

4. In this clip, who passed the test and who failed? Why?

What surprised you?

Javier and Shane encountered similar tests—of integrity. Knowing what is right and actually doing it is the essence of integrity. We often use the word *character* to describe a person whose actions are consistent with the attitudes and motives of his heart. What he builds his life on is expressed in how he acts. There is no hypocrisy.

Javier and Shane chose different paths because of the foundation and priorities of their lives, and they ended up in vastly different places.

Integrity is the opposite of hypocrisy. It means being honest all the time and speaking the truth in your heart. It means being the same person in secret as you are in public. When your life matches your words, and the standards you set for others are those you unashamedly live by as well—that's integrity. People of integrity treat others with kindness, just as they want to be treated. They cannot be bought or bribed.

God is true and there is no darkness or hypocrisy in Him (see 1 John 1:5-7). He calls us to be true as well.

Read Matthew 23:1-14,23-26.

5. **What did Jesus say that hypocrites need to do? (See v. 26.)**

To be clean both inside and out is the reason we should search our lives and hearts and ask God to cleanse us from any lack of integrity. Then we should begin to take steps to eliminate all hypocrisy from our lives. Hypocritical Christians turn people away from God while Christians of true integrity draw people to Him.

Let's each commit to start being the real deal—in the eyes of God and others—and to be an example for the world and our children.

6. **On the next page, circle attitudes and actions from Psalm 15 that represent a life of true integrity.**

"LORD, WHO CAN DWELL IN YOUR TENT?
WHO CAN LIVE ON YOUR HOLY MOUNTAIN?
THE ONE WHO LIVES HONESTLY, PRACTICES
RIGHTEOUSNESS, AND ACKNOWLEDGES THE TRUTH
IN HIS HEART—WHO DOES NOT SLANDER WITH HIS
TONGUE, WHO DOES NOT HARM HIS FRIEND
OR DISCREDIT HIS NEIGHBOR, WHO DESPISES THE
ONE REJECTED BY THE LORD BUT HONORS THOSE
WHO FEAR THE LORD, WHO KEEPS HIS WORD
WHATEVER THE COST, WHO DOES NOT LEND HIS
MONEY AT INTEREST OR TAKE A BRIBE AGAINST THE
INNOCENT—THE ONE WHO DOES THESE THINGS
WILL NEVER BE MOVED." PSALM 15

7. What does "The Two Tests" movie clip show you about being a role model for your children?

BLESSED CHILDREN

Many books, speakers, and events attempt to help parents keep their children happy. No one wants a screaming toddler or a defiant teenager, but do you know what will make your children really happy?

Read Proverbs 20:7-10 below.

"THE ONE WHO LIVES WITH INTEGRITY IS RIGHTEOUS; HIS CHILDREN WHO COME AFTER HIM WILL BE HAPPY. A KING SITTING ON A THRONE TO JUDGE SIFTS OUT ALL EVIL WITH HIS EYES. WHO CAN SAY, 'I HAVE KEPT MY HEART PURE; I AM CLEANSED FROM MY SIN'? DIFFERING WEIGHTS AND VARYING MEASURES— BOTH ARE DETESTABLE TO THE LORD." PROVERBS 20:7-10

8. **According to this passage if a person lives with integrity, his children will be blessed or happy. Specifically, why do you think this would cause a child to experience joy?**

According to verse 10, God hates "differing weights and varying measures." In ancient times, merchants priced goods based on the good's weight. Deceitful merchants would modify the actual weights of judgment so that the buyer would have to pay more than what the product was worth.

9. **How do the varying standards in verse 10 relate to standards parents set for themselves or for their children? Name some specifics.**

To live with integrity, we must humble ourselves, admit we don't have it all together, and ask God to give us wisdom each day to make the best decisions possible. When we do, He promises He will pour it on us "generously" and not make us feel foolish for asking (see Jas. 1:5).

"IF ANY OF YOU LACKS WISDOM, HE SHOULD ASK GOD, WHO GIVES TO ALL GENEROUSLY AND WITHOUT CRITICIZING, AND IT WILL BE GIVEN TO HIM." JAMES 1:5

Also, whether fighting off an unhealthy habit or seeking direction concerning finances, we should not be afraid to ask for help from other trusted people. Everyone needs answers and clarity. And victory comes to those with many advisors (see Prov. 24:6).

How can this group help you walk in integrity?

"A HOUSE IS BUILT BY WISDOM, AND IT IS ESTABLISHED BY UNDERSTANDING; BY KNOWLEDGE THE ROOMS ARE FILLED WITH EVERY PRECIOUS AND BEAUTIFUL TREASURE." PROVERBS 24:3-4

If your group is coed, you might consider moving into separate men's and women's groups now for a time of personal and family application.

SELF-EVALUATION

10. **Would you be proud of your children if they repeated your example in the following areas? Why or why not?**

Purity?

Language?

Choice of friends and recreational activities?

Devotion to the church and level of participation?

Love and respect demonstrated to your spouse?

Prayer life?

Biblical knowledge?

11. By your example in the home, how would your children describe your devotion to God? To the church? To your spouse? To them?

12. Of what inconsistency in your life do you need to repent and confess to your family?

SELF-EVALUATION

10. Would you be proud of your children if they repeated your example in the following areas:

Purity?

Language?

Choice of friends and recreational activities?

Devotion to the church and level of participation?

Love and respect demonstrated to your spouse?

Prayer life?

Biblical knowledge?

11. **By your example in the home, how would your children describe your devotion to God? To the church? To your spouse? To them?**

12. **Of what inconsistency in your life do you need to repent and confess to your family?**

This personal journaling section allows you to begin to set in place some important personal and family commitments. Activities can be done at the end of each session in your group or you can do them on your own.

What adjectives would people in your home, workplace, community, or church use to describe you?

Whatever you wrote above is your reputation.

What adjectives would God use to describe you?

Whatever you wrote here is your character. If these two lists don't match up, you may have an integrity issue.

What areas do you need to work on this week related to your integrity?
(For example, work on a habit you need to change, evaluate the movies your family watches, and so forth.)

How will you begin?

Do you have someone who can help you stay accountable?

COMMIT TO MEMORY

> "Why do you call Me 'Lord, Lord,' and
> don't do the things I say?"
> LUKE 6:46

A PRAYER FOR COURAGE

Dear Consistent Father,

You are who You say You are. You are consistent, steady, and faithful. I am so unlike You. I allow the stress of my day to affect my devotion to You. I allow the temptations of this world to determine my dedication to my family. I allow my mood to alter my worship. I allow distractions to keep me from what is most important.

Forgive me. I want what people say about me and what You say about me to match. I want to walk with integrity. I want to call You Lord and live in a way that is obvious You are my Lord. For Your glory and for the sake of the generations to come, make me a person whose talk matches my walk. Allow my family to see the best that I offer.

Amen.

COURAGEOUS HOMEWORK

The Resolution for Men, read:
- ☐ "Resolve to Love Your Wife" (pp. 87–99)
- ☐ "Resolve to Fight for Justice" (pp. 131–43)

The Resolution for Women, read:
- ☐ "My Integrity" (pp. 145–62)

OPTIONAL READING

SIX MARRIAGE ESSENTIALS

While rearing our children must be a priority, we must never forget that one of the greatest things we will ever do for our children is to love our spouse. The love children see between their parents should be so sacrificial and vibrant that they could never imagine settling for anything less when they look for a mate.

When a couple first signs that marriage license, marriage couldn't seem to be any easier. Young and in love, everything is perfect in the world; that is, until you really get to know each other. As the years go by, you learn so much about each other and about marriage, often by trial and error. Once a husband and wife become parents, an even greater responsibility exists.

So how should we keep our marriages healthy? How can parents grow in sacrificial love? While this isn't an exhaustive list, here are six marriage essentials for spouses to consider *together*.

1. Mutual Motivation. For a couple to succeed, spouses must possess mutual motivation. They must be in agreement about what the desired result of marriage looks like. If you look to the pages of Scripture, a worthy goal is *not* to get along peacefully, bring up children to be respected members of society, or purchase that pristine home in the suburbs.

Your goal as Christian parents must be to show the glory of God. When a couple desires above all for God to be pleased with all aspects of their home, then that mutual motivation settles most other issues that arise (see Eph. 5:22-25).

2. Deep Dialogue. Some conversations in marriage are reduced to simple fact inquiries: "How was your day?" "Did you pay the bills?" "Did you put the clothes in the dryer?" For a marriage to thrive, you must enter into deep dialogue. This type of communication involves both listening and speaking (see Jas. 1:19).

As children enter the scene, parents need to establish rules that children cannot interrupt Daddy and Mommy's time to talk. You two were together before they were around and, if you want to still be together once they are out of the nest, you must practice open, honest, deep dialogue.

3. Gracious Giving. If either person wakes up wondering what the spouse can do for him or her, then the day is off to a dangerous start. For a marriage to thrive, both parties must be committed to gracious giving. This takes place when a spouse decides to give of himself without any thought of return—a picture of unconditional love and unconditional service (see Col. 3:12-19). You choose to serve your spouse with a gracious attitude regardless of the response you may receive.

4. Controlled Calendar. Romance, nurture, and communication take time. Don't prioritize your schedule; instead, schedule your priorities (see Eph. 5:15-17). If you don't schedule what is most important to you, then someone or something else will do so for you. When that happens, your spouse normally gets the leftovers.

Having a controlled calendar might mean fewer hours spent on a hobby, fewer activities for your children, or actually having to say no to good causes for your family in order to maintain an intimate marriage relationship.

5. Fair Fighting. All couples fight, but few fight well. Scripture tells us to be angry, but we are not to sin in that anger (see Eph. 4:26). Unfortunately, our spouses often see our worse side, but we can change that.

Establish the rules for peacemaking when conflicts arise. Everyone has areas that we think are out of bounds in conflicts. It might be out of bounds for you or your spouse to walk away during a conflict, raise your voice, bring up past transgressions, involve other parties, or something else. Communicate with your spouse about how you can fight well when you fight.

6. Prioritized Passion. You will talk, share, and enjoy life with many people but you should only be having sex with your spouse. As life gets more hectic, it is easy to stop viewing this part of the marriage as important. Prioritized passion means ensuring that this part of your relationship be kept vibrant and fresh. Scripture tells us to take care of our spouse's sexual needs in order to avoid temptation (see 1 Cor. 7:3-5).

How do you rate yourself on these six essentials?

SERVING AND PROTECTING

THE MEASURE OF A MAN IS DETERMINED BY WHAT HE IS WILLING TO SACRIFICE FOR HIS FAMILY.

"Don't be afraid of them. Remember the great and awe-inspiring Lord, and fight for your countrymen, your sons and daughters, your wives and homes."

NEHEMIAH 4:14

THE WEEK IN REVIEW

Men, does your love for your wife weaken when she lets you down? Or does it stay rock solid in the midst of marital storms?

What injustice in your community calls for a courageous stand?

In *The Resolution for Women*, Priscilla Shirer states, "Instead of being repulsed by certain behaviors and grieved at the lies being foisted on our generation, we find ourselves more accepting of them, willing to watch and laugh, considering them suitable viewing with a side of popcorn" (p. 148). Indicate some specific behaviors she might have in mind.

1. Share a memory or two about special meals in your family (Thanksgiving, Christmas, etc.). Who usually does the serving?

In February 2006, a 41-year-old mother named Lydia Angyiou from Ivujivik, Canada, caught sight of an 8-foot, 700-pound polar bear making its way toward her 7-year-old son. She rushed to the polar bear and began to punch and kick until her children were safe and a neighbor came out with a rifle to finish the job. A witness described Lydia as "about 5-foot-nothing and 90 pounds on a wet day." Suffering minor injuries, she was able to protect her children.[1] Her children rarely rebel against her parenting anymore!

Stories like this one always get our attention. From time to time, we hear reports of a parent picking up a car when a trapped child is underneath. People debate encounters when adrenaline propels someone to do something superhuman.

More than likely, your family will encounter obstacles even more dangerous than an animal attack or a carjacking.

2. To what lengths would you go to protect your loved ones from an intruder?

Hopefully, you wouldn't stop at any cost. Yet, there is an enemy even more cunning and diabolical than any burglar, and he is coming for your loved ones. What are you willing to do to protect your family and provide them what they need?

3. How do you think most fathers would say that they serve and protect their families?

What do you think God looks for in a father who serves and protects his family?

Just as a community depends on law enforcement officers, knowing they will always be there, even in dangerous and life-threatening situations, so does a courageous father instill confidence in his family. His wife and children know that no matter what, they will never go without what they truly need.

Are you willing to rise to God's standard of serving and protecting your family?

83

STAKEOUT

INTENSE CONCENTRATION ON THE SUBJECT

A FATHER'S PROVISION

As the apostle Paul gave instructions to the church, he included instructions concerning families. You might be surprised at what he had to say.

Read 1 Timothy 5:8.

What are the implications of this verse for fathers?

COURAGEOUS CLIP

Watch *COURAGEOUS* Clip 7, "Javy's Provision." Discuss using activity 4.

→ **All video clips are available for free at lifeway.com/courageous**

4. Based on his actions, what do we know about Javy as a father?

> "DO NOTHING OUT OF RIVALRY OR CONCEIT, BUT IN
> HUMILITY CONSIDER OTHERS AS MORE IMPORTANT
> THAN YOURSELVES. EVERYONE SHOULD LOOK OUT
> NOT ONLY FOR HIS OWN INTERESTS, BUT ALSO FOR
> THE INTERESTS OF OTHERS." PHILIPPIANS 2:3-4

Javy wanted and needed a job; he had a natural desire and motivation to take care of his family and meet their needs. This faithful father accepted the responsibility God had entrusted to him, knowing God would lead him every step of the way.

A FATHER'S PROTECTION

Not only are fathers called to provide, they also are called to protect. While financial security is important, fathers protect their families in other ways.

The Israelites were exiled from their land. Nehemiah sought God's help through prayer and fasting and regrouped the people to come back and rebuild the wall (approx. 445 B.C.; chaps. 1–3). While rebuilding, the people faced physical and verbal persecution from those who would halt God's work. Watching his countrymen lose heart before his eyes, Nehemiah made a drastic move to ensure the completion of the wall.

Read Nehemiah 4:10-15.

5. What did Nehemiah do to ensure that the wall would be completed?

How did this change the perspective of the workers?

Nehemiah reminded the people of two things: (1) the greatness of their God and (2) the reason they were fighting—for their families (see v. 14). By stationing men by their families in exposed areas of the wall, the veracity of their fight was completely parallel to their love for their families. If there ever was a time to fight, it was then; their families' lives depended on it. And your family's lives depend on such a stand today as well.

6. **Where are some exposed areas in the walls of homes today?**

COURAGEOUS CLIP

Watch and debrief *COURAGEOUS* clip 8, "Nathan Protects His Home."

➔ **All video clips are available for free at lifeway.com/courageous**

7. **From what things was Nathan trying to protect his daughter?**

The Resolution for Men (pp. 229-30) lays out six powerful influencers we must monitor and guard in our children's lives. Each of them can greatly impact their thinking and decisions.

1. Their friends
2. Their education
3. Their music
4. Their movies/TV shows
5. The Internet
6. Video games

Are you allowing anything in your home or family that could destroy the purity, conscience, or mind of your spouse or children?

We should teach our children to ask, "Is this honoring to God?" "Is this true, holy, and healthy?" "Will this help me to do the right things?" "Will this make me love God more?" "Will this fuel my passion for Christ, or will it pour cold water on it?" Romans 12:21 urges, "Do not be overcome by evil, but overcome evil with good."

A FATHER'S ATTITUDE

8. Read Psalm 23. How does the shepherd protect and provide for his sheep?

God fathers us like a shepherd. He cares for His flock, and He knows us personally. He makes us lie down when we are weary and He provides His presence as our protection (see Ps. 23).

One of the ways Jesus described Himself was as the Good Shepherd. He knows us and we know Him. No enemy has a chance to get to us since He will lay down His very life to protect and care for us (see John 10:11).

If your group is coed, you might consider moving into separate men's and women's groups now for a time of personal and family application.

A FATHER'S PROVISION

9. **Circle ways that fathers are to provide for their families:**

Physical Necessities   Emotional Love/Affection

A Spiritual Example   Clear Direction

Boundaries/Guidelines   Prayer/Counsel

If you circled them all, then you are absolutely right! In what ways are you currently succeeding in providing for your family?

Where could you improve? Write your responses below or on a separate piece of paper.

A FATHER'S PROTECTION

10. **Where are the exposed areas in your home? Be specific as you identify dangers for each family member.**

What are you going to do practically to protect your family?

10-4 WOMEN
HEARING AND ANSWERING THE CALL

A MOTHER'S PROVISION

9. **Circle ways that parents are to provide for their families:**

Physical Necessities   Emotional Love/Affection

A Spiritual Example   Clear Direction

Boundaries/Guidelines   Prayer/Counsel

Where could you improve?

In what ways does your husband succeed in providing for your family? How often does he hear how much you appreciate his efforts?

A MOTHER'S PROTECTION

10. **Where are the exposed areas in your home? Be specific as you identify dangers for each family member.**

What are you going to do practically to protect your family?

This personal journaling section allows you to begin to set in place some important personal and family commitments. Activities can be done at the end of each session in your group or you can do them on your own.

One of the greatest ways you can protect your family is by protecting yourself. Where are you under attack? How will you avoid or tear down areas of danger starting this week?

If you fall morally, how are your children affected?

What does it mean that Jesus cares for you as the Good Shepherd? How will you begin to care for your family this way?

COMMIT TO MEMORY

"Don't be afraid of them. Remember the great and awe-inspiring Lord, and fight for your countrymen, your sons and daughters, your wives and homes."
NEHEMIAH 4:14

A PRAYER FOR COURAGE

Dear Jesus the Messiah,

Your sacrificial example takes my excuses away. I want to lay down my life for my family. I will be the first to do without. I will be the first to serve. I will be the first to sacrifice.

May I be the first to rise and the last to sleep. Let my knees be the first thing to hit the ground in the morning, entrusting my family to Your sufficient care. Let them see clearly that my source of strength is Your Word.

Give me grace to live with my family as I serve them and protect them. Grant me the privilege to work harder than anyone else in order to care for them. And bless me with the opportunity to pray over them while they sleep.

Make me more like Jesus and equip me to die to myself, take up my cross daily, and follow You in all my ways.

Amen.

COURAGEOUS HOMEWORK

The Resolution for Men, read:
- ☐ "Resolve to Demonstrate Love" (pp. 145–55)
- ☐ "Resolve to Provide for Your Family" (pp. 157–67)

The Resolution for Women, read:
- ☐ "Authentically Me" (pp. 49–65)
- ☐ "My Blessing" (pp. 111–26)

CEO DAD VERSUS SHEPHERD FATHER

"You're fired!" Donald Trump's famous line from his reality TV show has become a cultural icon. With little remorse, he tells contestants how far off the mark they are, sending them to the streets jobless.

This type of ruthless business management makes it into the home as well. Sometimes unknowingly, results-oriented fathers may show their approval when a job is well done but humiliate or discourage when a task is subpar. Men are wired to expect results, and that is not a bad thing in and of itself. That tendency turns bad when fathers have high expectations and look for results without modeling love for their children.

This outcome is why the apostle Paul taught, "Fathers, don't stir up anger in your children, but bring them up in the training and instruction of the Lord" (Eph. 6:4). In an attempt to instruct their children, many fathers would unfortunately frustrate if they stirred up their children to anger out of a results-oriented mind-set.

God fathers us not as a CEO, but as a Shepherd. He cares for His flock. He makes us lie down when we are weary, and He provides His presence as our protection (see Ps. 23). With Him watching over us, no enemy has a chance to get to us since He is willing to lay down His life to protect us (see John 10:11). He carries us through those wilderness places in our lives as the supreme example of a protective father (see Deut. 1:30-31).

It is true that all fathers are to receive their example concerning fatherhood from God Himself (see Eph. 3:14). At times frustration become necessary for the flock; at times approval causes jubilation. Regardless of the situation, God as Shepherd proves faithful in His long-suffering concerning us.

At times you too will become discouraged. You may think your instruction is going in one ear and out the other one. Imagine how often God has felt the same way toward us. But as your Father and Shepherd, He stays faithful.

Will you remain faithful for your wife and children? Exemplify long-suffering and patience? Lay down your life for your family?

BOYS VERSUS GIRLS

It doesn't take children long to figure out that there are differences between genders. For some reason, when we become parents, we forget those differences altogether.

The Bible speaks to differences between men and women and we would be wise to keep those uniquenesses in mind. As you rear boys and girls, we are growing them into men and women of godly character.

Differences in Roles. Men are called to be the head of the family (see Eph. 5:23); women are called to be the helper (see Gen. 2:18). Both roles are important and both roles are different.

The uniqueness of God's punishments when Adam and Eve sinned speaks to the difference in roles. God promised that women would have an ongoing struggle concerning who was in charge within the marriage relationship (see Gen. 3:16). He cursed Adam with difficult labor due to the fact that Adam "listened to your wife's voice and ate from the tree about which I commanded you, 'Do not eat from it' " (Gen. 3:17).

Differences in Traits. A main goal of this study is to highlight God's purposes for men in their homes. Men are called to lead (see Eph. 5:23), to sacrifice (see Eph. 5:25), and to provide (see 1 Tim. 5:8). While children are to honor both parents, the apostle Paul singled out fathers to be a patient teacher of their children (see Eph. 6:2-4).

Scripture affirms the contributions of a capable and godly wife (see Prov. 31:10-31). Women are called to help (see Prov. 31:11-12), to submit to their husbands out of respect for the Lord (see Col. 3:18), and to care for the needs of their homes. They are to live in ways that show and teach younger women how to love their husbands and children (see Titus 2:3-5).

Differences in Needs. God's commands and the differing needs of men and women underscore their unique roles. Women are called to submit to their husbands (see Eph. 5:22), many of whom long for significance and someone to recognize their achievements. Little boys who are told what they are good at often grow up to be men who are confident in how God has wired them.

Men are called to love their wives in a sacrificial manner (see Eph. 5:25), and women long for the security that comes from someone always willing to give of himself. Little girls who find their security in Christ and what a real godly man lives like will rarely settle for anything less.

SECURING YOUR HOME

If you live in a dangerous neighborhood, more than likely you make every effort to protect your home and family. Whether it is installing a dead bolt lock, purchasing a security system, or taking some other action, it makes sense to secure your home in a dangerous environment.

We live in a very dangerous world in which many forces endanger our children. The only problem is, walls can't stop these intruders. The rise of media influence gains ground by the day; the problem is, most children are smarter with technology than their parents. Most parents are unaware that secret codes are often used to keep snooping parents at a distance (for example, *CD9, Code 9* which means parents are around; *NIFOC*—naked in front of computer; *S2R*—send to receive pictures; etc.).

At the risk of seeming uncool to your children and their friends, you must take drastic measures to keep your children safe. Any attempt to provide a fail-safe plan will be outdated almost immediately, but here are a series of questions to constantly ask yourself:

What type of access do my children have? Just because their friends have certain types of technology does not mean you must provide those things for your child. While centralized computers and televisions may seem archaic, if you want to protect your children, start by eliminating constant access.

How knowledgeable am I concerning the content they see? Most teen dramas promote sexual activity, sexual exploration, and substance abuse. If your children cannot watch a show with you, they shouldn't watch it at all.

Who are my kids' friends? Whether they have friends next door or online, you need to be aware of the relationships that are influencing your children (see Ps. 1:1-2). You have the right to ask about their 972 friends on Facebook. You also have the right to open their account and "defriend" suspicious "friends."

Who is teaching them sex education? The classroom provides one type of education, and their classmates "teach" another type. Unfortunately, the learning age gets younger all the time. Your children are being filled with lies. Are you teaching them the biblical truth about sex?

Can I monitor their activity? The very fact your child would explode if you asked for a password shows why you need one. So much text messaging and social networking takes place in a private world. What are you doing to monitor what your child is receiving and what your child is initiating?

WINNING
AND BLESSING
THEIR HEARTS

BEFORE YOU CAN SPEAK
TO THE HEARTS OF YOUR CHILDREN,
YOU MUST FIRST WIN THEIR HEARTS.

"My son, give me your heart,
and let your eyes observe my ways."
PROVERBS 23:26

THE WEEK IN REVIEW

In *The Resolution for Women*, Priscilla Shirer recalls a time she chose an item for her office and built her workspace (and life) decorating around it. She learned, "We need to figure out what to do with the house before we decide where to put the accessories" (p. 53). Good advice for parents, too.

How have you, unintentionally perhaps, picked up bits and pieces from the world and built your thoughts and parenting around them?

Dads, are you known for loving others? As a praying father?

Will you take the risk of asking your wife and kids how you're doing as a provider?

1. **Every generation is given an example in movies or television of what fathers are like. What famous personality represented fatherhood for your generation? What were his top five characteristics?**

Hollywood continues to portray deadbeat dads and men in general as clueless and worthless. Even when dads approach a tender moment in a movie or TV show, most characters return to their selfish ways, much to the amusement of the audience. Fathers are a laughingstock in our culture.

When you think about fathers today, you may automatically associate them with characteristics like the ones you discussed. Dads themselves may be starting to assume that such portrayals are the norm. It is past time to develop a new perception *for* fathers and a new view *of* fathers.

2. What man in your life has best represented biblical fatherhood for you? What are his top five characteristics?

People of faith recognize that God has a good and noble role for fathers to fill. While the man you described above is not perfect, he impacted you and spoke into your life in positive ways. He certainly has made and may be continuing to make an impact on his children. Even if his children ultimately make unwise decisions, they cannot use their father as an excuse to not follow God.

3. To what voices are your children listening right now?

How can you win and bless your children's hearts so they listen to your voice?

If we truly care that our children succeed at following God, we will stop at nothing to ensure that we win their hearts.

STAKEOUT

INTENSE CONCENTRATION ON THE SUBJECT

AFFIRMING YOUR CHILDREN

You cannot speak into the hearts of your children if you don't have their hearts. To learn how to win their hearts, let's learn from God, the Father.

In Matthew 3:13-17, John the Baptist baptizes Jesus to inaugurate His ministry. In this moment, we gain insight into the Trinity's work (seeing all three present; Father, Son, and Holy Spirit) and also see a beautiful affirmation from our Heavenly Father. As you read and listen, realize that this passage is a picture of God affirming Jesus, not establishing Him. There is an important difference.

Read Matthew 3:16-17 below and look for ways that the Heavenly Father affirmed Jesus.

"AFTER JESUS WAS BAPTIZED, HE WENT UP IMMEDIATELY FROM THE WATER. THE HEAVENS SUDDENLY OPENED FOR HIM, AND HE SAW THE SPIRIT OF GOD DESCENDING LIKE A DOVE AND COMING DOWN ON HIM. AND THERE CAME A VOICE FROM HEAVEN: THIS IS MY BELOVED SON. I TAKE DELIGHT IN HIM!" MATTHEW 3:16-17

---

4. **What specifically do you see in verse 17?**

The Father's words at Jesus' baptism reveal three affirmations:

1. The Father was honored to call Jesus His Son.
2. He loves His Son very much.
3. God was pleased with how His Son was living on earth.

"THEN A VOICE CAME FROM THE CLOUD, SAYING:
THIS IS MY SON, THE CHOSEN ONE; LISTEN TO HIM!"
LUKE 9:35

Also at Jesus' transfiguration, in Luke 9:35, the Father stated emphatically that people should listen to His Son, indicating that Jesus was of such stature ("Chosen One") that others would benefit from knowing and hearing Him. God reiterated His special relationship with Jesus ("My Son").

As in the baptism account, God affirmed Jesus so others could hear. The Father told Jesus that He loved Him in a sincere and passionate way.

Every child desires to hear these affirmations in a similar spirit:

1. You are loved.
2. You make me proud.
3. You are good at ...

5. **What is the most impactful thing your father ever told you? (Even if it was not positive, sharing shows how important this is for you.)**

6. What do you think your children are longing to hear from your lips?

What is holding you back from saying it to them?

COURAGEOUS CLIP

Watch *COURAGEOUS* clip 9, "A Better Brother." Discuss using activity 7.

→ **All video clips are available for free at lifeway.com/courageous**

7. From this scene, what did Dylan know about his parents' feelings toward him?

8. What is the difference between saying you love someone and giving him your approval?

What does it mean to you when someone tells you "I love you" or "I'm proud of you"?

Some children have never heard either from their parents. Others have vivid memories of a parent telling them, "I'm proud of you." Perhaps that affirmation is more specific, acknowledging your child's priceless worth.

MODELING FOR YOUR CHILDREN

In the last verse of the Old Testament, the prophet Malachi told the people of the forthcoming Jesus. Through the work of John the Baptist and Jesus, a specific action would take place; otherwise, God's curse would fall on the people. Read the verse below.

"HE WILL TURN THE HEARTS OF FATHERS TO THEIR CHILDREN AND THE HEARTS OF CHILDREN TO THEIR FATHERS. OTHERWISE, I WILL COME AND STRIKE THE LAND WITH A CURSE." MALACHI 4:6

One outcome of Christ's coming ministry was to bring fathers' hearts back to their children and children's hearts back to their fathers.

As we win our children's hearts, what are we called to do with them?

Read Proverbs 23:26 (see p. 95).

9. What is the good and the bad of a child's being told to "observe my ways"? (Also see 1 Cor. 11:1.)

Not only are we called to win our children's hearts, but once we have won them, we must instruct them in the right way to live.

COURAGEOUS CLIP

Watch *Courageous* clip 10, "Nathan's Date with Jade." Discuss this clip using activity 10.

➔ **All video clips are available for free at lifeway.com/courageous**

10. How do you think this dinner affected Jade's future decisions?

At a pivotal time in Jade's life, Nathan spoke truth over her in a life-changing way. Recognizing the opportunity he had, he expressed his love, affirmation, encouragement, and hope for her future. Nathan both told and showed Jade how much he loved her and was proud of her.

He presented Jade with a wonderful reminder of the love of both of her parents. Nathan promised their lifelong support and discipleship of Jade as a godly woman while at the same time calling her to stand for God, honoring herself and her future husband.

Parenting roles change as children mature, as this clip illustrates well. For their own safety, toddlers benefit more by a loving authority figure than they do by a loving counselor—more appropriate when children are about to leave the nest, like Jade.

No matter their age or life stage, your children will always need your love, encouragement, and affirmation. Let them know it, hear it, and see it.

"THE BLESSINGS OF YOUR FATHER EXCEL THE BLESSINGS OF MY ANCESTORS AND THE BOUNTY OF THE ETERNAL HILLS." GENESIS 49:26

To win and bless the hearts of your children—what does it look like? Your children know that you love them and have their best interests in mind; you affirm them for who they are as unique individuals; and they trust and allow you to speak value and success into their lives, as Nathan did with Jade.

Such parents encourage in both word and in deed. Leading humbly and gratefully, they are both disciples and disciplers, starting at home.

If your group is coed, you might consider moving into separate men's and women's groups now for a time of personal and family application.

AFFIRMING YOUR CHILDREN

11. **If someone interviewed your children and asked how you felt about them, what do you think they would say?**

In the space below, write each child's name. Under each name, list all the great qualities you see in that child.

When and how do you plan to tell them, "You are loved, you make me proud, and you are good at (_____those items listed above_____)"?

MODELING FOR YOUR CHILDREN

Often parents have lost their children's hearts by wounding them. A parent's anger, hypocrisy, harshness, or lack of time and affection can cause a son or daughter to withdraw emotionally. Ephesians 6:4 warns fathers against provoking their children to anger.

12. Write each of your children's names below and evaluate them based on the following questions. Talk with your spouse about her responses.

Name of child	_____	_____	_____	_____
Do I have this child's heart?	YES	YES	YES	YES
	NO	NO	NO	NO
Does he/she respect me?	YES	YES	YES	YES
	NO	NO	NO	NO
Does he/she listen to me?	YES	YES	YES	YES
	NO	NO	NO	NO
Does he/she want to be around me?	YES	YES	YES	YES
	NO	NO	NO	NO
Have I wounded him/her in any way?	YES	YES	YES	YES
	NO	NO	NO	NO
Does he/she believe he/she has my heart?	YES	YES	YES	YES
	NO	NO	NO	NO

Malachi 4:6 says that the parent's heart should turn first toward their child. It's time to check your priorities, and do whatever it takes to win your child's heart back. If you have wounded them, then apologize. If you don't have time for them, then be open to making some needed schedule changes.

What do you plan to do in the next few days to win the hearts of your children and to instruct them in ways to help guard their hearts?

AFFIRMING YOUR CHILDREN

11. **If someone interviewed your children and asked how you felt about them, what would they say? What would they say about their father?**

In the space below, write each child's name. Under each name, list all the great qualities you see in that child.

When and how do you plan to tell them, "You are loved, you make me proud, and you are good at (_____ those items listed above_____)"?

MODELING FOR YOUR CHILDREN

Often parents have lost their children's hearts by wounding them. A parent's anger, hypocrisy, harshness, or lack of time and affection can cause a son or daughter to withdraw emotionally. Ephesians 6:4 warns fathers against provoking their children to anger.

12. **Write each of your children's names below and evaluate them based on the following questions. Talk with your spouse about his responses.**

Name of child	_____	_____	_____	_____
Do I have this child's heart?	YES	YES	YES	YES
	NO	NO	NO	NO
Does he/she respect me?	YES	YES	YES	YES
	NO	NO	NO	NO
Does he/she listen to me?	YES	YES	YES	YES
	NO	NO	NO	NO
Does he/she want to be around me?	YES	YES	YES	YES
	NO	NO	NO	NO
Have I wounded him/her in any way?	YES	YES	YES	YES
	NO	NO	NO	NO
Does he/she believe he/she has my heart?	YES	YES	YES	YES
	NO	NO	NO	NO

What do you plan to do in the next few days to win the hearts of your children and to instruct them in ways to help guard their hearts?

This personal journaling section allows you to begin to set in place some important personal and family commitments. Activities can be done at the end of each session in your group or you can do them on your own.

Proverbs 23:1-26 contains wise sayings by which a child could learn from observing his father's ways. Read these verses this week.

If you have children at home, calculate how many months they have left at home. Write that number beside each child's name below.

While they will always be your children, the time and opportunity to mold their lives is passing quickly. Write plans to start this week, month, and year with each child to make sure you are winning his or her heart.

THIS WEEK

THIS MONTH

THIS YEAR

COMMIT TO MEMORY

"My son, give me your heart,
and let your eyes observe my ways."

PROVERBS 23:26

A PRAYER FOR COURAGE

Dear Heavenly Father,

I desire my children to have Your absolute best. I don't want them to fill up on the scraps of this world and miss being truly satisfied in the feast You provide. This world is at war for the souls of my children. I cannot keep my children out of the world, but I can fight to keep the world out of my children.

I need Your help to win their hearts. I need them to hear me teaching Your ways, and I need them to see me living according to Your ways. My time is running out. I am not promised tomorrow, so help me to awaken today from any complacency, tiredness, and selfishness. Allow me to see my children as the precious gift they are from You.

I declare war today on those things that lure my children away from You, and I will fight for them by the strength and grace You provide.

Amen.

COURAGEOUS HOMEWORK

The Resolution for Men, read:
- [ ] "Resolve to Bless Your Children" (pp. 101–13)
- [ ] Invest in some heart-to-heart time with each child this week.

The Resolution for Women, read:
- [ ] "It Only Works When I Breathe" (pp. 105–10)
- [ ] "Loving My Children" (pp. 205–26)

OPTIONAL READING

BLESSING YOUR CHILDREN (What Does That Mean?)

Jacob provides the most descriptive example in Scripture of a father blessing his children (see Heb. 11:21). Nearing death, he gathered his family together and blessed each of his sons and also his grandsons who were fathered by Joseph. In this time, men would bless others by prophesying over them concerning future blessings. This could include praying to God on behalf of the person being blessed.

Most of the time, the future blessing was given in regard to past behavior. Often, a faithful son received a promising blessing. An ungodly son received a dreadful blessing.

When a father gathered the family together to pronounce blessings, both positive and negative moments were relived. In the case of Jacob, he reminded Reuben of his sexual immorality and Simeon and Levi of their violent anger (see Gen. 49:3-4,5-7). He praised Joseph for his fruitfulness and steadiness (see vv. 22-24). With such verbal blessings, a gift of land was often distributed. The weight of these blessings was felt deeply because the prophecy surpassed the son's life, on to his descendants.

While biblical prophecy occasionally ventured into set days or events, the prophets usually presented messages similar to those a parent would deliver to a child. "If you continue to do this, your future will look like …" "If you don't stop, I'm going to have to discipline you." Prophecy usually addressed the natural progression of a person or people concerning their obedience or disobedience.

Apply that to Jacob's blessing, and we understand more clearly. Simeon was a violent man. Jacob discerned that in his son and prophesied that violence was in Simeon's future (see v. 7). From Jacob's example, we learn that fathers are to bless children with appropriate words and gifts.

Appropriate Words. Blessing a child with appropriate words means telling the truth. "Whoever speaks the truth declares what is right, but a false witness, deceit" (Prov. 12:17). Fathers are not to enable children for continual disobedience.

If your children are walking down a path that leads to destruction, the best blessing you can give them is to tell them of looming danger. Conversely,

111

if your children are walking faithfully in the Lord tell them of the great joy they give you (see Prov. 10:1).

Appropriate Gifts. Jacob played favorites with his sons. While his extreme favoritism with Joseph caused family drama (see Gen. 37:3-4), Jacob still resolved to give gifts of land to his sons in a way he deemed appropriate. Normally, the more trustworthy the son, the more generous the gift. Jacob had experienced so much of God's gracious provision that he did not want to see it thrown away by unreliable sons.

The Blessing on Jesus. The idea of a father's blessing is not as prominent in the New Testament due to the church's functioning as the people of God. In these pages the best example of a father blessing his son is evident in Jesus' baptism.

Within the pages of Scripture, biblical blessings happened at pivotal moments (near a father's death, baptism, etc.). God chose to bless His Son at a pivotal time. Coinciding with His inauguration into ministry, Jesus traveled to the Jordan River so John the Baptist, His cousin, could baptize Him (see Matt. 3:13). "After Jesus was baptized, He went up immediately from the water. The heavens suddenly opened for Him, and He saw the Spirit of God descending like a dove and coming down on Him. And there came a voice from heaven: This is My beloved Son. I take delight in Him!" (Matt. 3:16-17). At the transfiguration, the disciples heard the Father say, "This is My beloved Son. I take delight in Him. Listen to Him!" (Matt. 17:5).

Through the Father's words, we see how a father should bless his child in three specific ways: acceptance, adoration, and approval.

Acceptance—The Father wanted listeners to know that Jesus was *His* Son. Fathers show their acceptance by addressing children according to who they really are, not who they desire them to be.

Adoration—God had no problem telling the world that He adored Jesus. As a beloved Son, Jesus knew that His Father was crazy about Him and didn't care who knew it. Fathers should express the type of love that treasures their children and delights in them.

Approval—Not only did God tell people that He accepted and adored Jesus, He also wanted all to know that He approved of Him. He told the disciples to listen to what His Son had to say. When a father tells a child that he is good at something and everyone should know and benefit from it, few compliments in this life will ever surpass this one.

LEAVING
A LEGACY

NO ONE LEAVES A GODLY LEGACY BY ACCIDENT.

"We must not hide them from their children, but must
tell a future generation the praises of the LORD, His
might, and the wonderful works He has performed."
PSALM 78:4

THE WEEK IN REVIEW

In what ways did heart-to-heart time with your children bless you as much as it did them?

Do you find yourself experiencing any of the heart hindrances described in "How Fathers Lose Hearts"? (*The Resolution for Men*, pp. 106–9)?

Which do you desire more: to be your child's friend or to be your child's parent? How does this affect the way you parent?

No matter their size, most churches have some ministries by which they serve the community and Christ.

1. **List three ministries of your church or a church with which you're familiar. In a sentence, describe the purpose of each ministry.**

Most churches create ministries so an unmet need can be addressed. Due to a dire budget situation, someone recommends that a tithing ministry be created—and those involved are the only ones who are doing all the giving.

Is this ministry a good idea or a bad one? Why?

It is the privilege and responsibility of every believer to give God "the firstfruits of all your increase" (Prov. 3:9-10, NKJV) because the Bible teaches it; to count on a tithing ministry to fill the gap would be a bad idea. Each believer is accountable to God.

In your list, you might have identified children's ministry or youth ministry. So what is the purpose of each one? Quite possibly, people might assume that it is the church's job to teach your children about God. If that is your understanding, then it is unbiblical!

Many parents expect the church to do all the work associated with their children's spiritual upbringing. Parents' general attitude toward being involved in their children's lives may consist of connecting their children with qualified professionals and then stepping out of the way. Due to strong children's ministry in many churches, some parents have eased into complacency regarding their children's spiritual development.

Does this mean your church shouldn't have ministries gearing toward your children? Absolutely not! But churches and families need to rethink their partnership.

2. Practically, what is the difference between these two statements: (a) We desire parents to support the children's ministries of this church, or (b) Our ministry purpose is to support the role of parents.

The Bible is unashamedly clear: Parents, particularly fathers, are ultimately responsible for the biblical education of the next generation. Your job is to leave a godly legacy to your children.

You cannot leave a godly legacy by accident.

115

STAKEOUT
INTENSE CONCENTRATION ON THE SUBJECT

A TEACHING FATHER

Standing upon the cusp of entering the promised land, Moses gathered the nation of Israel for final instructions before embarking on their long-awaited entry. After 40 years of wandering, the people were finally ready to inherit the land. At this critical juncture, Moses recapped Israel's history and reminded the people of God's commands.

Before they entered the land, Moses instructed the people regarding one of their greatest responsibilities of all.

Read Deuteronomy 6:4-9.

3. **Moses gave God's people some specific instructions in these verses. What were they?**

How often were the people to teach their children about God's love?

How does this biblical model contrast with what many families experience today?

While on earth, Jesus invested in twelve ordinary men whose lives were transformed by knowing Him personally. Jesus spent time with them. He called them to exchange the ordinary for the extraordinary. He taught them about God and His Word, and He showed them how to pray.

Jesus healed their family members. He served, rebuked, and forgave. He modeled God's love. In the Great Commission, Jesus called us to make disciples and so share in His work.

"GO, THEREFORE, AND MAKE DISCIPLES OF ALL
NATIONS, BAPTIZING THEM IN THE NAME OF THE
FATHER AND OF THE SON AND OF THE HOLY SPIRIT,
TEACHING THEM TO OBSERVE EVERYTHING I HAVE
COMMANDED YOU. AND REMEMBER, I AM WITH YOU
ALWAYS, TO THE END OF THE AGE." MATTHEW 28:19-20

Our obedience to be a disciple and make disciples starts at home, with those who are closest to us.

How seriously have you taken God's calling for you to help win your children to Christ and then teach them to love God with all their hearts? This is not rocket science. It is simply talking with your children during the day about God and about your heart's desire for them to love and obey Him.

COURAGEOUS CLIP
Watch *COURAGEOUS* clip 11, "Adam and Dylan Run" and debrief.

→ **All video clips are available for free at lifeway.com/courageous**

4. **What teachable moments in this clip gave you hope?**

Even though Adam didn't start well, he acknowledged that fact to his son and resolved to finish better. He wanted more for Dylan and for himself.

A FATHER FIGURE

An increasing number of children are growing up in fatherless homes. Even when fathers are present physically, they are not always spiritual role models.

If your family faces that situation, take comfort in knowing that Timothy, one of the early church's pastors, did so as well. It appears that Timothy's father was not a man of faith (see Acts 16:1-3), but he was blessed to have godly maternal influences and a father figure in the apostle Paul.

Read 2 Timothy 1:3-7.

5. **What did you notice about Paul's relationship with Timothy? About Timothy's family relationships?**

Even though Timothy was in a less-than-ideal situation, God equipped him to be a mighty man of faith. Now that you understand this dynamic, read on.

Read 2 Timothy 2:1-2.

What was Paul hoping his investment in Timothy would produce?

Timothy's connection to Paul as a "spiritual father" came through his relationship with Jesus. A beautiful aspect of the body of Christ is that children who do not have fathers or godly father-figures can be welcomed into the church. Suddenly they have many fathers and are a part of many families who will train and mentor them.

You may visit church occasionally and sit on the back row, but are you really plugged in and involved? One of your homework readings this week

(p. 202, *The Resolution for Men*) highlights four ways for families to better enjoy and get involved in the body of Christ.

Once you are plugged in, then look around and ask God to help you reach out in love as a "father figure" or "spiritual mom" to those who don't have fathers.

As the *COURAGEOUS* movie concludes, a montage of fatherhood scenes dramatically reminds the viewer of the impact of godly fathers and families.

What do you think is happening in this scene?

Derek's association with a gang took him on a dangerous path and landed him in the wrong place—jail.

6. In your opinion, how good are Derek's chances to succeed in life as an inmate?

While we don't know all that the situation entails, we do know a good deal about Nathan. His decision to mentor Derek improves Derek's future chances immensely.

Who has God placed in your life who needs your love and influence?

If your group is coed, you might consider moving into separate men's and women's groups now for a time of personal and family application.

A TEACHING FATHER

7. On a scale of 1 to 10, with *10* being *best prepared*, how equipped are you to teach the Bible to your children?

How concerned are you that your children follow the Bible?

Even if you don't feel equipped, if you are truly concerned for your children, you will do whatever it takes to teach your children to love the Lord.

For example, if you decided to homeschool your children tomorrow, you wouldn't need to master all the material from kindergarten-12th grade at one time. Instead, you would concern yourself with enough information to get started for tomorrow. That's all you have to do here!

With no preparation or training, many parents disciple their children by reading God's Word out loud to them in the morning or at night and then talking with them about what they read. It's very simple and can make all the difference in the world.

Moses and Joshua did not feel equipped to lead a nation, but God used both men mightily. Being available and obedient was the first step.

8. What could you teach your children today about God, His love, His Word, and other spiritual matters? How would you teach them?

A FATHER FIGURE

9. In your sphere of influence, are there young people you know who may need a positive family role model? Write their names below and what each child appears to need most from a father figure.

10. What can you do this week to reach out to those children and be a Paul to them? Talk with your wife about her thoughts on this lesson.

A TEACHING MOTHER

7. On a scale of 1 to 10, with 10 being best prepared, how equipped are you and your husband to teach the Bible to your children?

How concerned are you that your children follow the Bible?

Even if you don't feel equipped, if you truly are concerned for your children, you will do whatever it takes to teach your children to love the Lord.

For example, if you decided to homeschool your children tomorrow, you wouldn't need to master all the material from kindergarten-12th grade at one time. Instead, you would concern yourself with enough information to get started for tomorrow. That's all you have to do here!

With no preparation or training, many parents disciple their children by reading God's Word out loud to them in the morning or at night and talking with them about what they read. It can make all the difference in the world.

Queen Esther did not feel equipped to lead a nation, but God used her "for such a time as this" (Esth. 4:14). Being available and obedient was her first step.

8. What could you teach your children today about God, His love, His Word, and other spiritual matters? How would you teach them?

How will you support your husband in his efforts to make such a commitment to your family?

A ROLE MODEL

9. In your sphere of influence, are there young people you know who may need a positive family role model? Talk with your husband about how you both answered this question.

As a seller of purple, Lydia exerted influence in the community. When she came to faith in Jesus, her household also believed and was baptized (see Acts 16:13-15). She worshiped God and opened her home to other believers (see Acts 16:40).

10. What would it look like for you and your husband to commit your home to being a safe, open place for your children and their friends? What would that decision teach your children?

TAKE THE WHEEL

RETAKING LEADERSHIP WITH YOUR FAMILY

This personal journaling section allows you to begin to set in place some important personal and family commitments. Activities can be done at the end of each session in your group or you can do them on your own.

What is your plan to truly grow in knowing God's Word and applying it to your life and home?

This week watch for teachable moments with your children and the "Timothys" who come your way. Some of these times will come about naturally, but others you will have to create.

How do you plan to instill a love for God in them this week?

Psalm 78:1-8 is a great guide. It tells us that parents should teach children two things: (1) how good God has been and (2) where previous generations have messed up.

How could you use a process like this to disciple your family?
I do, you watch
I do, you help
You do, I help
You do, I watch

COMMIT TO MEMORY

"We must not hide them from their children,
but must tell a future generation the
praises of the LORD, His might, and
the wonderful works He has performed."
PSALM 78:4

A PRAYER FOR COURAGE

Dear God of Truth,

I hate how Your Word is devalued in our society, but I hate even more how Your Word has been devalued in my life. I want to love You with all my heart, soul, and might for my benefit but also so my children will have that model burned into their minds.

I treasure the attempts my church makes to teach my children, but they were never intended to take my rightful job. I will be responsible for setting the standard my children have concerning how to love You. I will not expect someone else to do my job.

I also pray that You equip me to invest in fatherless children while ever increasing in the teaching of my own children for the sake of the next generation of believers. I want to live in a way that all the children within my influence will be able to understand the love of You, their perfect Father. Help me to live a legacy that outlives me.

Amen.

COURAGEOUS HOMEWORK

The Resolution for Men, read:
- [ ] "Resolve to Live with Honor" (pp. 115–29)
- [ ] "Resolve to Leave a Legacy" (pp. 211–22)

The Resolution for Women, read:
- [ ] "Leaving a Godly Legacy" (pp. 247–66)

As a couple, read page 202, *The Resolution for Men* and discuss the four keys to being successful in how you plug into a church.

OPTIONAL READING

THE FAMILY ALTAR

In a time when few families watch TV together, eat a meal together, or share a Saturday playing games together, the thought of worshiping together may seem like a far-fetched goal. Culture bombards us with the notion that children need to be independent and have room to develop on their own. Children use the overstated line that their friends get certain privileges and they need them as well. What transpires is family members isolating themselves in different rooms of the house without any discipling interaction.

If you think your children would balk at the thought of your family gathering together for worship on a regular basis, then that is all the more urgent reason to start such a time. The term *family altar* speaks to a time when the leader of the home gathers the family together to focus on God. For some families, that may happen once a week, perhaps Saturday evenings as the family prepares to worship with their church family on Sunday or as a new week begins. Other families practice this time every day at the breakfast table or through nighttime prayers.

Why is a family altar important? God says so, that's why! Here are just a few of the examples of God's stance on the family altar. Abraham was told to teach his children so that the generations that followed would know the Lord (see Gen. 18:19). Moses taught that parents were to teach their children to love the Lord throughout the day (see Deut. 6:7).

The psalmist taught the necessity of God's people declaring God's greatness to the next

generations (see Ps. 78:1-7). In Proverbs 22:6, Solomon taught that when a child is trained in the Lord, he or she will not depart from that way. Fathers are to teach their children the instruction of the Lord (see Eph. 6:4).

What should you do when everyone is together for family worship?

1. Read. Get into the Bible together. Help children know how to look up verses. Let them participate by sharing, reading, or responding to stories. Do all family members own a personal Bible?

If you don't know the Bible well yourself, then begin by staying one step ahead of your children. You will learn as you teach them. For young children of differing ages, you might use children's Bibles, but it is very helpful to read chronologically. Often children are only taught stories and don't see the big picture. Resources like *The Big Picture Storybook Bible* or *The Jesus Storybook Bible* can help.

If your church has a reading plan for studying the Bible or a Bible book, then that provides another great option. Check *Read the Bible for Life* as a chronological reading plan *(www.lifeway.com/readthebibleforlife)*. Also, Lifeway Sunday School curricula for both adults and children offer family worship ideas that support study themes.

One way to help children begin to put God's Word in their hearts is through Scripture memory. Challenge all family members to learn a family verse, and encourage everyone to memorize age-appropriate verses. Make it fun and another means of helping your family view the Bible as a special Book and source of practical daily guidance and wisdom.

2. Pray. Don't rush through prayer, and creatively and appropriately try to involve everyone. Ask for prayer requests from your family. Get in a circle and ask each person to pray for the person on his or her right. Set a prayer focus for each day (Sunday-church leaders, Monday-friends, Tuesday-missionaries, etc.). Use this time to work on family dynamics that need the Lord's guidance. Share God's answers to these prayers.

3. Worship. Even if you don't play an instrument or sing well, you can lead your family in worship. Sing a cappella or along with a CD. If you have a family musician, stir up that gift (see 2 Tim. 1:6). Children love making and playing instruments as they sing.

Don't expect the church or another person to do what God has called and equipped you to do. Disciple your family!

10 COMMANDMENTS OF SINGLE PARENTING

Parenting with a dedicated spouse alongside you is difficult enough. When a person has to go it alone, the challenges increase greatly. So how is a single parent to go about the difficult duties of raising children? While it is difficult to give advice that applies to every situation, there are some common recurring issues.

1. Thou shalt not bash your ex-spouse. No divorce has ever been one-sided. The only way it could be is if one of the spouses were perfect (and Jesus never got married). Even if your ex-spouse is far from God, he or she has a pivotal role in your child's life. Don't use words for evil (see Jas. 3:6).

2. Thou shalt not bash your child's stepparent. Your best efforts can be spent praying for, rather than bashing, that person (see Prov. 10:19). Your child's stepparent will never replace you, but it might backfire if you stoop to attacks.

3. Thou shalt not be afraid to ask for help. Regardless of the reason you are a single parent, you don't need to remain isolated. God has put the church in place to help in areas in which we are weak. Don't assume someone knows you need help. Ask for it.

4. Thou shalt not settle for less than God's best. Worse than being a single parent is to marry an ungodly person in order for your children to have a "replacement" parent. Don't make that mistake (Prov. 26:11). Too often, single parents drown in parental pressure and decide to settle for lower standards than what they know is God's best. Trust God, not your emotions!

5. Thou shalt not live in the past. The past is in the past. Keep it there! The pain you experienced is real, but God is able to carry you forward, and God's people are there to comfort you (see Deut. 1:30-31; 2 Cor. 1:3-5).

6. Thou shalt not use your children for revenge. Unfortunately, your children may have had to go through the pain that led to a single-parent family. Don't add pain on top of that by using them as ammunition against the one who hurt you. Your time would be better spent repairing the hurt that was done to your children (see Prov. 14:26).

7. Thou shalt not be overwhelmed with guilt. We all have mistakes in our past, but if we have experienced godly grief that leads to repentance, we should not have regret (see 2 Cor. 7:10). Those of us in Christ are no longer condemned, so we should not continue to live in shame (see Rom. 8:1).

8. Thou shalt not overcompensate with your children. Often parents feel so sorry for children in single-parent situations that they enable them to bad behavior. You are called to raise your children in the instruction of the Lord (see Eph. 6:4).

Don't let the past give them a free pass for future ungodly living. Gifts cannot replace what they lost. Stay committed to being a godly parent.

9. Thou shalt not believe that you are a second-rate family. While you are at a disadvantage, you are not second rate. Many of Scripture's heroes came from less-than-ideal homes, and God dwells with those in unfortunate family situations (see Ps. 68:5).

10. Thou shalt trust the Lord with all your heart. As you walk this journey, remember Proverbs 3:5-6: "Trust in the LORD with all your heart, and do not rely on your own understanding; think about Him in all your ways, and He will guide you on the right paths."

Surrounding Yourself with Accountability

THE PEOPLE CLOSEST TO YOU
MUST BE CLOSEST TO GOD.

"Iron sharpens iron, and one man sharpens another."
PROVERBS 27:17

1. **Milestones mark our lives (major decisions, experiences with God, marriage and children, accomplishments, losses, etc.). Share where you were when a memorable milestone occurred for you.**

In the past seven weeks, we have covered some heavy situations. Many of us are choosing to replace fear and passivity with courage and direction.

2. **What has impacted you most?**

How has going through this study with a group improved your efforts?

Our appreciation of law enforcement officers has grown as well. They face all types of danger, often having to call for backup in order to stay safe in a hostile situation.

3. **For what situations do officers need to request backup?**

What spiritual backup would benefit you once this study concludes?

THE WEEK IN REVIEW

The Resolution for Men describes a father's godly legacy in this order: first as a faithful follower of Christ, second as a faithful husband, third as a faithful father, and then as a strong spiritual leader in the world (p. 212). To what extent are these in the right order for you?

How would teaching your children to fear the Lord impact your parenting? (See pp. 117-18, *The Resolution for Men.*)

What are some choices you will make in the next few days, weeks, or months that provide you the opportunity to impact your legacy?

The insights we have discovered together over these weeks can continue to be life changing. While you may be committed and on track today, a time will come when your motivation diminishes and you need someone to push you onward again. Tests and temptations will come. If you want to be courageous for the long haul, you must surround yourself with accountability.

In order to succeed, those closest to you must be close to God. Of course, you will always reach out to those far from Jesus; but if you want to stay faithful to God and your family, you must surround yourself with people who have the same life goal.

If your motivation is to last longer than this study, then you must commit yourself to taking next steps.

**ACCOUNTABLE *adj.*
subject to giving an account: answerable**

STAKEOUT
INTENSE CONCENTRATION ON THE SUBJECT

ACCOUNTABLE FIRST TO GOD

The Bible is full of teachings regarding the people you need in your life and those you should avoid.

4. As different people read these verses aloud, write what the Bible teaches you regarding relationships.

Psalm 1:1-3

Proverbs 13:20

Proverbs 27:17

1 Corinthians 15:33

Galatians 6:1-2

5. Concerning those who might walk away from being courageous, how do Jesus' instructions in Matthew 18:15-20 help us stay accountable?

Why do you think we hesitate to follow these instructions?

COURAGEOUS CLIP

Watch *COURAGEOUS* clip 12, "Resolution Ceremony." Discuss this clip using the next question.

→ **All video clips are available for free at lifeway.com/courageous**

6. In this scene of resolve, to whom were Nathan and the other fathers answering, or giving an account?

These fathers had supported each other in the past; in what ways would you expect them to encourage each other in the future?

What challenges do you think might come your way after this study?

How will each of you be able to help one another?

ACCOUNTABLE TO EACH OTHER FOR THE LONG HAUL

Make no mistake, distractions intent on luring us away are already nearing. So what will it take for us to make it in the long haul?

Read Hebrews 10:24-25 below and underline key phrases.

"LET US CONSIDER ONE ANOTHER IN ORDER TO STIR UP LOVE AND GOOD WORKS, NOT FORSAKING THE ASSEMBLING OF OURSELVES TOGETHER, AS IS THE MANNER OF SOME, BUT EXHORTING ONE ANOTHER, AND SO MUCH THE MORE AS YOU SEE THE DAY APPROACHING." HEBREWS 10:24-25, NKJV

7. **What does verse 25 mean when it says "not forsaking the assembling of ourselves together"?**

To what two things are we called to "stir up" one another?

Good accountability is about being a true Christian friend. It means comforting someone when he is down, encouraging her to do the right thing, praying for protection and guidance for your friend, and even lovingly reproving when he or she gets off track. Accountability is helping someone be found faithful to God!

As you can see, we need each other. Not just during these few weeks, but long term, throughout our lives. God never intended for any of us to live the Christian life alone. As the body of Christ, we are to work together and share our lives together for the sake of God's kingdom and for the sake of our children and the many generations to come. By God's grace, we will be found faithful to His calling! May the apostle Paul's affirmation below be true for each of us!

"I HAVE FOUGHT THE GOOD FIGHT, I HAVE FINISHED THE COURSE, I HAVE KEPT THE FAITH; IN THE FUTURE THERE IS LAID UP FOR ME THE CROWN OF RIGHTEOUSNESS, WHICH THE LORD, THE RIGHTEOUS JUDGE, WILL AWARD TO ME ON THAT DAY; AND NOT ONLY TO ME, BUT ALSO TO ALL WHO HAVE LOVED HIS APPEARING." 2 TIMOTHY 4:7-8, NASB

WE ARE MORE ACCOUNTABLE NOW

In Luke 12:47-48 Jesus taught that people who know and better understand what God requires of them are more accountable than those who do not (also see Eccl. 5:4-5, Jas. 3:1-2). Each of us is more accountable now—doubly accountable, to God and to each other—because of what we have learned during our time together in these sessions.

If your group is coed, you might consider moving into separate men's and women's groups now for a time of personal and family application.

DOUBLY ACCOUNTABLE

8. Of all that we have learned, for what three things do you need the most encouragement, prayer, and accountability in the next month?

What is the best way to keep you accountable (style and method such as meet for coffee, e-mail, etc.)?

9. Read 1 Corinthians 10:12-13. In what areas are you concerned you might fall?

"WHOEVER THINKS HE STANDS MUST BE CAREFUL NOT TO FALL. ... HE WILL NOT ALLOW YOU TO BE TEMPTED BEYOND WHAT YOU ARE ABLE, BUT WITH THE TEMPTATION HE WILL ALSO PROVIDE A WAY OF ESCAPE SO THAT YOU ARE ABLE TO BEAR IT."

1 CORINTHIANS 10:12-13

---

10. How does the promise of verse 13 encourage you?

10-4 WOMEN
HEARING AND ANSWERING THE CALL

DOUBLY ACCOUNTABLE

8. Of all that we have learned, for what three things do you need the most encouragement, prayer, and accountability in the next month?

What is the best way to keep you accountable (style and method such as meet for coffee, e-mail, etc.)?

9. Read 1 Corinthians 10:12-13. In what areas are you concerned you might fall?

"WHOEVER THINKS HE STANDS MUST BE CAREFUL NOT TO FALL. ... HE WILL NOT ALLOW YOU TO BE TEMPTED BEYOND WHAT YOU ARE ABLE, BUT WITH THE TEMPTATION HE WILL ALSO PROVIDE A WAY OF ESCAPE SO THAT YOU ARE ABLE TO BEAR IT."
1 CORINTHIANS 10:12-13

---

10. How does the promise of verse 13 encourage you?

This personal journaling section allows you to begin to set in place some important personal and family commitments. Activities can be done at the end of each session in your group or you can do them on your own.

> "WHOEVER THINKS HE STANDS MUST BE CAREFUL NOT TO FALL." 1 CORINTHIANS 10:12

As we conclude this study, it is time to set some things in place to ensure success. It has been said that we all have fallen in the past, we all are about to fall presently, and we all have ways we can fall in the future.

For what things in the past do you need to ask forgiveness from God?

We all are one decision away from ruining our lives. Is there anything in your life right now that you need to confess to God and one accountability partner?

How can you best set yourself up to not fall in the future? Be specific.

COMMIT TO MEMORY

"Iron sharpens iron, and one man sharpens another."
PROVERBS 27:17

A PRAYER FOR COURAGE

Dear Steadfast Father,

I want to be relentlessly courageous but not blindly overconfident. My family is too precious for me just to hope I will finish strong based on my own efforts. I need Your help. Please help me to love You more every day and to teach my children to follow You with their lives. With Your Spirit walking alongside me, I beg you to send me others who have courageous hearts and who want the same things I do—to live a life pleasing to You.

I cannot make it on my own. Please help me align my life so that the people closest to me are closest to You. Let us spur one another on to love and good deeds. When we fall, let us show grace. When we slow down, let us push one another on. And when we walk away from You, let us turn one another back in order that we not settle for anything less than Your best.

You deserve it. My spouse deserves it. And my children and the next generations need it.

Amen.

COURAGEOUS HOMEWORK

The Resolution for Men, read:
☐ "Resolve to Be Found Faithful" (pp. 197–209)
☐ "Appendix 5: Resolution Groups:
Accountability for Men" (pp. 235-37)

The Resolution for Women, read:
☐ "Faithfully His" (pp. 67–85)
☐ "My Best" (pp. 89–110)

OPTIONAL READING

NEXT STEPS

What an incredible eight weeks! We pray that you have grown so much during the days of *Honor Begins at Home* that your family, church, and community are all reaping the benefits. Can you imagine what would happen in our world if fathers lived up to the calling of God on their lives?

So, now that the study is over, where do you go from here? The real work is just beginning. If you really want to finish fatherhood strong, you are going to have to focus on relationships. Five key ones are identified below.

Develop an action plan for these relationships. Include the act of asking someone to hold you accountable as you take these steps.

1. Relationship with God. Apart from Christ, you can do nothing (see John 15:4). Without a growing relationship with God, your efforts will be in vain. He is "your life" (Col. 3:4), "shield" (Ps. 18:2), "strength" (Ps. 28:7), and "power" (2 Cor. 12:9). Get in His Word and pray daily.

Your Plans:

2. Relationship with Accountability Partners. This study's effectiveness had a lot to do with how well and how honestly your group interacted. "Iron sharpens iron" (Prov. 27:17), and we are called to spur one another on to love and good deeds (see Heb. 10:24-25).

Continue meeting with this group, start another group, or grab an accountability partner to meet with weekly as you hear and do God's Word (see Jas. 1:22). This relationship will help turn the zeal you are experiencing now into actual implementation of life change.

One of the readings this week in *The Resolution for Men* ("Resolution Groups: Accountability for Men") describes some of the dynamics of an accountability group—what you can expect and how you might contribute.

Available Opportunities:

3. Relationship with Your Spouse. Don't try to make these changes without the support of your spouse. Ask forgiveness for times you have fallen short in the past and share how you plan to change things now. Make it a point weekly to nurture your marital relationship.

Your Plans:

4. Relationship with Your Children. Don't neglect the future due to shame from the past. Regardless of how you started, finish well. Make a plan on how you are going to start investing yourself in the life of each child.

If you need to apologize to your children, don't let pride stop you. Share with them your resolve to change and tell them it's because you want Jesus to change your home.

Your Plans:

5. Relationship with Your Parents. We have covered the need to forgive those in the past who have hurt us, but if you haven't gotten there yet, you must take this step of obedience if you want to live courageously. Making your children pay for the hurt your parents caused you can easily happen. For your children to have the best, you need to redeem your past.

Your Plans:

A NEW LIFE

The Bible tells us that our hearts tend to run from God and rebel against Him. The Bible calls this "sin." Romans 3:23 tells us, "All have sinned and fall short of the glory of God." Every lie, bitter response, selfish attitude, and lustful thought separates us from God. We all deserve His judgment. Even though you deserve judgment, God loves you and wants to save you from sin and offer you a new life of hope. John 10:10 states, "I [Jesus] have come so that they may have life and have it in abundance."

To give you this gift of salvation, God made a way by sending His Son, Jesus Christ. Romans 5:8 tells us, "God proves His own love for us in that while we were still sinners, Christ died for us!" You receive this gift by faith alone. Ephesians 2:8 confirms, "You are saved by grace through faith, and this is not from yourselves; it is God's gift."

Faith is a decision of your heart demonstrated by the actions of your life. Romans 10:9 says, "If you confess with your mouth, 'Jesus is Lord,' and believe in your heart that God raised Him from the dead, you will be saved."

The Bible commands everyone to repent and to believe in the Lord Jesus Christ to be saved. If you choose right now to believe that Jesus is God's Son, that He died for your sins, and that by believing you receive new life through Him, consider praying a prayer like this:

"DEAR GOD, I CONFESS THAT I AM A SINNER AND THAT MY SIN SEPARATES ME FROM YOU. I BELIEVE JESUS DIED TO FORGIVE ME OF MY SINS. I ACCEPT YOUR OFFER OF ETERNAL LIFE. THANK YOU FOR FORGIVING ME OF ALL MY SIN AND GIVING ME MY NEW LIFE. FROM THIS DAY FORWARD, I WILL CHOOSE TO FOLLOW YOU."

Share your decision with a Christian friend or pastor. If you are not already attending church, find one that preaches the Bible and will help you worship and grow in your faith. Following Christ's example, ask to be baptized by immersion as a public expression of your faith.

Group Leader Tools

- *Honor Begins at Home* member book for each attendee
- Teaching Clips available for free at lifeway.com/courageous
- Copies of *The Resolution for Men* and *The Resolution for Women* (available at lifeway.com/courageous)
- Bibles for each attendee

Begin in prayer for yourself, for families, for parents and children, and for the people who will attend. Pray for spiritual protection. If your church is conducting a Courageous campaign, plug into the prayer guide. Or in the four weeks leading up to this study, pray for vision (see Phil. 3:13-14); pray for possibilities and protection (see Eph. 3:20); pray for families (see Deut. 6:6-9); and pray for children (see Phil. 2:14-15).

Watch the movie if you've not already. Read the Bible study, and watch the appropriate clips with each section. Do the readings recommended for participants. Secure a room and equipment, and work with the group promoting this study. Familiarize yourself with the list of registrants.

Keep in mind these characteristics of a good leader:

- You can never transform a life; only God can through His Holy Spirit. If He has called you to facilitate a group, trust Him to help you lead it.
- Your sessions should feel more like a conversation than a classroom experience. Be careful not to say something like: *Now we're going to answer question 1.*
- Remember, a great group leader talks less than 10 percent of the time. Don't be afraid of silence.
- Each session contains more material than you can use in an hour. To accomplish all parts of a session, ideally a group will have 90 minutes. The activities that are **numbered and boldface** are basic to the study; secondary or follow-up questions can be eliminated if your time is limited. Many numbered activities are self-explanatory and easy to use. Subsequently not every activity is addressed in the leader guide.

Prepare for each session in advance so you can be responsive to your group's needs and the Holy Spirit's leadership. Whatever your choice, value your attendees' time. At the same time, remember that people and their needs are far more important than completing all the questions.

Bonus footage such as "Desperate Parenting" (3:43) and others referenced in this guide can (1) help you anticipate issues that might arise with the group, (2) use parts in a session as time allows, or (3) enhance personal preparation and encouragement. This footage, along with all the other clips are available for free at lifeway.com/courageous

SESSION SCHEDULE

BRIEFING (Icebreaker, 10–15 min.)—An atmosphere of fun and sharing helps participants get to know each other and move into the topic.

Beginning in session 2, this segment also includes review of readings from *The Resolution for Men* and *The Resolution for Women*. Several questions will be offered; choose one or two for your group.

STAKEOUT (Bible study, 50 min.)—During this time, the group begins to grapple with what God's Word says on the subject. Movie clips are part of this segment. Be sensitive to anyone who is not familiar with the Bible, church, or prayer, perhaps pairing him or her with a church member.

10-4 MEN and 10-4 WOMEN (Application, 20 min.)—Some coed groups will want to remain together to make family applications, while others may move into separate men's and women's groups. Activities are provided for both situations; if a coed group stays together, use the 10-4 Men page. Or break into gender groups for several sessions but not all.

Another option is to discuss the *Resolution* readings by gender groups. Discern the needs of your group and do what works best for participants.

TAKE THE WHEEL (Commitment and closure, 5 min.)—This is a call for men to take leadership of the family. Activities include journaling, a verse to memorize, a prayer for courage, and assignments during the week. Some of this content is best prayed over and fully processed throughout the week.

"A Prayer for Courage" is not intended to be a prescribed prayer but a framework to use. Hopefully, you will have some participants not accustomed to praying who may benefit by seeing a printed example.

SESSION 1
Accepting Your Responsibility

COURAGEOUS clip 1, "Not Good Enough" (5:08) and clip 2, "Adam's Speech" (3:19)

→ **All video clips are available for free at lifeway.com/courageous**

Unless you meet in advance, you will need to highlight small-group processes and values, distribute resources/take up money, and handle other logistics in session 1.

BRIEFING—To encourage serious conversation, start with safe conversation. Icebreakers help loosen everyone up, get your group talking, and set up discussion. Allow people to think but jump-start the conversation by sharing an idea or two, especially at the beginning of your study or if people don't know each other.

Icebreaker option: If a reality TV show were following your family around for a week, what would they see? Of what things would you be proud? Embarrassed about?

Elaborate on how we often spend a lot of time on the house and less on the people inside it. Instruct the group to write their responses to the "successful parenting" question **(activity 2)** and call for one or two answers. (The theme of success as a dad/parent runs throughout this study; definitions of successful parenting hopefully will change.) TIP: When people write their answers, they are more apt to share.

Be encouraging, no matter the answer. At this point, as hearts are turning toward the subject matter, pray that God would raise up courageous fathers and families.

STAKEOUT—Show *COURAGEOUS* **clip 1, "Not Good Enough" (5:08),** which reveals how many dads view their roles and responsibilities. Debrief as a group using **activity 3**.

Summarize the content leading up to **activity 4**. Instruct group members to read Joshua 24:14-24 and to do **activities 4–5** on their own. Assure everyone that there is no right or wrong answer to **activity 5** and that responses will not be shared.

Transition: *In addition to considering a father's choice, we also must understand a father's biblical charge.* Direct the group to Ephesians 6 for what God expects of fathers; ask someone to read verses 1-4 aloud. Read the "Paul exhorts ..." paragraph aloud (p. 16); ask participants to reread the verse on their own before doing **activity 6**.

Unpack both parts of **activity 7** as a large group, listing all practical and specific actions the group suggests. Show *COURAGEOUS* **clip 2, "Adam's Speech" (3:19),** to challenge, motivate, and set the big picture of fatherhood as God intended.

10-4 MEN and 10-4 WOMEN—If desired, divide into separate gender groups to enable sharing. Throughout the study the same male group leader should guide the men's group and the same female leader, the women's group.

TAKE THE WHEEL—You may want to vary whether journaling is done in class or during the week. As *Resolution* readings increase, participants may appreciate making application during the session when Bible study is fresh.

Overview the *Resolution* books and purposes by saying: The Resolution for Men, *by Stephen and Alex Kendrick, screenwriters of* COURAGEOUS, *strategically inspires men to reconcile with their past, reengage in the present by taking full responsibility for their wives and children, and move forward with a bold, clear resolution for the future.*

Written in partnership with the movie, Priscilla Shirer's The Resolution for Women *will inspire a resolution revolution. Like the men in the movie who resolve to fully accept their responsibilities before God, Shirer explains how today's women can and should live out their own resolution.*

Distribute these books and explain how weekly readings enhance this study: *Beginning with session 2, we have a brief time to review.* Encourage spouses who are doing this study together. Dismiss by praying for your group.

SESSION 2
Embracing Your Identity

COURAGEOUS clip 3, "Gospel at Gun Range" (3:38)

→ **All video clips are available for free at lifeway.com/courageous**

Claiming their identity in Christ—accepting Him for the first time and/or committing to a growing relationship with Him and sharing their faith—must be the starting point and power behind everything parents do for their family. Without a relationship with Christ and His abiding presence, all efforts are in our own strength.

Participants will see in the movie clip a clear, relational, conversational presentation of the gospel and will talk about Scriptures that help them unpack God's grace. You will have the opportunity to share your testimony. Be sensitive to those who may need to test themselves "to see if you are in the faith. Examine yourselves" (2 Cor. 13:5). Be available if anyone needs to talk. Also, "A New Life" (p. 145) is a plan of salvation tool.

BRIEFING—Greet and welcome any newcomers. Share encouraging words heard about the study. Use **activity 1** to help the group build community.

This week is your first opportunity to help the group review between-session readings. (Possible answers, p. 67 in *The Resolution for Men,* one of seven principles Stephen and Alex Kendrick use to define manhood—an adult male who *accepts his masculinity; thinks and acts with maturity; embraces responsibility; functions independently; can lead a family faithfully; recognizes his accountability; is an image bearer of God)*

Using **activity 2**, point out the greater responsibility that is before fathers: *Worse than the possibility of physical harm coming to our children is spiritual harm. Our children are in danger and need the best type of protection possible.* As you finish, allow each person to pray for the individual on either side.

STAKEOUT—Make sure the group is looking for key phrases; then go through **activities 4–5** together. As needed, write the acrostic (God, Rebellion, Atonement, Conversion, Eternal Life) on a whiteboard so they can make notes.

Show **COURAGEOUS clip 3, "Gospel at Gun Range" (3:38)** and comment after viewing: *You just experienced an example of lifestyle evangelism. This scene happens in our day-to-day encounters with people, not in church.* Debrief the evangelistic nature of this clip using **activities 6–7;** unpack more about taking responsibility as a parent using **activity 8**.

Enlist someone to read Acts 26:1-23 aloud. Time the reader to see how long it took Paul to share his testimony here. Ask the group to share their testimonies with partners in the same amount of time or less **(activity 10)**. Be sensitive to anyone who may not have a testimony and be under conviction.

10-4 MEN and 10-4 WOMEN—Move into gender-specific groups at this time if this is your practice.

TAKE THE WHEEL—Allow time in the session for journaling if this is your practice. Close with "A Prayer for Courage" and an overview of readings in the *Resolution* books.

SESSION 3
Redeeming Your History

COURAGEOUS clip 4, "Nathan at Grave" (3:44) and clip 5, "David's Letter" (3:05)

➔ **All video clips are available for free at lifeway.com/courageous**

Optional video: In this study men and women will be discussing what it means to be a chain breaker and reading more about it in their *Resolution* books. This session introduces the idea of breaking the chains of your past and setting a new pattern of godliness. Redeeming family history is essential, though not easy or quick.

The bonus segment "Breaking the Chains" (3:17) features Sherwood Baptist Church leaders Stephen and Alex Kendrick, Jim McBride, and Michael Catt addressing this topic. Incorporate all or part of this video into a session if time allows. Or use for your personal preparation as a leader.

BRIEFING—Ask review questions to tap insights from the week's readings; affirm the group for their efforts. In advance ask a group member to pray for the group.

Question 2 gets deep quickly so set the tone. Remind people they are not to share every detail and that they don't have to share at all if they are uncomfortable. The goal is to give Jesus the glory, not the sin. After sharing and review, pray for the session.

STAKEOUT—Set up Matthew 18:21-35 as if Peter were excitedly setting a new standard. In that day, to forgive so much went far beyond what was practiced or expected. But Jesus' standard is always higher than our own. Ask a group member to read this passage.

Show *COURAGEOUS* clip 4, "Nathan at Grave" (3:44) and connect the movie clip to your discussion about forgiveness. Ask: *In what ways was Nathan a chain breaker?* Remind the group that while pain from the past is real, forgiveness is greater.

Ask another volunteer to read Romans 12:17-21 aloud and then reread Matthew 18:33-35 to reinforce: *You can pray and fully release your imperfect earthly father from any and all deep hurts he may have caused you in the past. You can do that now.* Use a poster sheet or other visual to compare godly and worldly grief **(activity 5)**.

Encourage men not to be overwhelmed by all they need or want to do. **Clip 5, "David's Letter" (3:05)** highlights starting where you are and taking one step at a time. Make sure the group identifies the different actions David took by writing this one letter.

Lift up the role of the men who supported David. Emphasize: *David's relationship with Christ also changed him as a father.*

10-4 MEN and 10-4 WOMEN—If men and women are meeting in gender-specific groups for application, how is discussion going? Hopefully the longer groups meet together and get to know each other, the more trust can be built and the more needs can be met.

TAKE THE WHEEL—Encourage journaling and actions during the week, including weekly readings in the *Resolution* books. Ask God to bless the homes that are represented.

SESSION 4
Walking in Integrity

COURAGEOUS clip 6, "The Two Tests" (4:50)

➔ **All video clips are available for free at lifeway.com/courageous**

BRIEFING—Have fun with **activity 1,** which helps the entire group relax, get better acquainted, and move into the topic. Your group is at the midpoint of *Honor Begins at Home* and should be experiencing more trust and openness.

Distribute the names of group members. Ask each participant to pray for that person in the coming week, that he or she will live a life of integrity. Include a time of silent prayer.

Before moving into **activity 2,** give a personal example you are comfortable sharing. Your willingness to share encourages everyone.

Choose a question or two to review the previous week's *Resolution* readings. Affirm the group for their commitment to their families.

STAKEOUT—Choose someone to read Luke 6:46-49 aloud. Before he or she reads, share: *Listen to these verses as if you are hearing them for the first time. Listen for the details of what Jesus was saying.* Compare and contrast the two houses Jesus referred to in this passage using **activity 3.** After participants share their ideas, transition into the next question by saying: *Storms raged against both houses. One man dug deep, building his home ...*

Show ***COURAGEOUS* clip 6, "The Two Tests,"** and debrief using **activity 4.** Discuss who passed and who failed their tests of integrity. Using the suggested passages from God's Word, compare and contrast integrity and its opposite, hypocrisy.

Using **activity 7** to consider what this movie taught about being a role model, consider the examples parents set for their children, whether they are aware of it or not.

Comment: *We all want our children to be happy, but for them to be truly blessed, parents must live lives of integrity.* Lead the group to experience and respond to principles from God's Word using **activities 8–9.**

10-4 MEN and 10-4 WOMEN—Doing **activities 10–12** for yourself and praying over them during the week will help group leaders be more open to God's leading in their group. Participants are moving into intense biblical content and self-examination, especially **activity 10.**

TAKE THE WHEEL—To review, highlight the difference between reputation and character (p. 76). Allow some time for journaling in the session if possible. Close by praying for families of integrity. Encourage group members in *The Resolution for Men* and *The Resolution for Women* readings.

Point out the optional reading by reminding parents that the best thing they can do for their children is to love and cherish their spouse.

SESSION 5
Serving and Protecting

COURAGEOUS clip 7, "Javy's Provision" (3:04) and clip 8, "Nathan Protects His Home" (1:47)

→ **All video clips are available for free at lifeway.com/courageous**

Optional video: The bonus segment "Taking Back the Home" (3:22) could be used effectively in this session. Either choose an appropriate portion for your session or use in personal preparation.

BRIEFING—To begin this week's group, ask each member to write down the names of their children. Then pass out the papers so everyone can pray for someone else's children during the week.

Emphasize: *The ways mentioned in response to* **activity 3** *are great things for fathers to do.* Show how we cannot neglect the most important thing for other good things as you proceed to the second part of **activity 3.**

STAKEOUT—Encourage your group to be honest in sharing all the implications related to 1 Timothy 5:8. You want them to come up with words like *hopeless, lost, selfish,* and so forth to show the weight of the message of this verse.

Set up the ***COURAGEOUS* clip 7, "Javy's Provision" (3:04)** by reminding the group of Javy's situation as an unemployed father desperately looking for a way to provide for his family: *Be on the lookout for his level of sacrifice for his family.* As you transition, highlight the importance of both providing and protecting: *Providing is giving a family what they need; protecting is safeguarding a family from what they do not need.*

The Nehemiah passage is a good visual transition into protecting the home and safeguarding the family. Talk about some of the exposed areas in the walls of many homes today using **activity 6.** Show ***COURAGEOUS* clip 8, "Nathan Protects His Home" (1:47)** and debrief with **activity 7**.

Pull out children's names from the opening prayer time. Enlist group members to ask out loud if someone would fight for his or her family (for example, Bill pulls out Tim's prayer card and asks, "Tim, how hard will you fight for Sarah and Jonathan?"). Continue as appropriate for your group size and dynamics. Or use in Take the Wheel.

10-4 MEN and 10-4 WOMEN—Encourage spouses to communicate with each other about their experiences in this study. Women are being encouraged this week to express gratitude to their husbands for efforts to provide for the family. Sometimes wives will be looking at their husband's responsibilities as well as at their own roles.

TAKE THE WHEEL—Emphasize how protecting your family starts with guarding your heart and avoiding danger yourself. Highlight *Resolution* readings this week. Spend time in prayer to close. Affirm participants for their participation and growth.

SESSION 6
Winning and Blessing Their Hearts

COURAGEOUS clip 9, "A Better Brother" (3:06) and clip 10, "Nathan's Date with Jade" (2:10)

→ **All video clips are available for free at lifeway.com/courageous**

Optional video: The bonus video segment "God's in Control of the Home" (3:05) could be used in this session if time allows. Sherwood leaders Michael Catt, Stephen Kendrick, Alex Kendrick, and Jim McBride dialogue about this topic. Or use in your personal preparation.

BRIEFING—Start this session by allowing a few men or couples to share how their homes are changing. Be prepared, if needed, to share an example.

Ask the group to write answers to **activity 2** before sharing answers together. This would be a great time for you to share about a man who exemplified godly characteristics for you. Tell the group of the impact he had on you and how you want to be that kind of model for your children.

STAKEOUT—Begin: *To win the hearts of our children, it's important to affirm them. In this section, we are going to look at how to truly do so.* As the group shares answers to **activity 4,** you will be able to categorize their responses in three ways:

1. You are loved.
2. You make me proud.
3. You are good at ...

Be sure to draw the application of our following God's example as a father. Show ***COURAGEOUS* clip 9, "A Better Brother" (3:06)** and ask: *How did Adam show he was proud of Dylan?*

In addition to affirming our children, we must also model for them what we expect from them. We want God's best for their lives so they need to see examples of how we are living according to God's best.

Set up **COURAGEOUS** clip 10, "Nathan's Date with Jade" (2:10), by reminding them that Nathan's daughter was being pursued by a boy who was in a gang. In an attempt to keep her safe from that attraction, he provided her the security of a father's love.

10-4 MEN and 10-4 WOMEN—Spend time looking at the great characteristics of your kids. Talk with your spouse regarding this list in **activity 11.**

TAKE THE WHEEL—Getting started requires looking ahead. Don't let participants be overwhelmed by being asked to start a monthly or yearly plan. To put one step in writing for each time frame can move most people to take huge strides forward.

Highlight the *Resolution* readings this week to encourage your group.

SESSION 7
Leaving a Legacy

COURAGEOUS clip 11, "Adam and Dylan Run" (2:26)

➔ **All video clips are available for free at lifeway.com/courageous**

BRIEFING—Remind the group that next week is the last session. If you are planning something special, communicate those plans here. Also, provide details concerning any upcoming resolution ceremony for your group and/ or church.

Make certain in this section to overemphasize that you are not downplaying church ministries, but you are simply putting them in proper context. They cannot do what parents are called by God to do. Show how the church and home need to partner.

STAKEOUT—Set up this clip by reminding participants that, early in the movie, Adam was a father too distracted to spend time with his son. Say: *Regardless of how you started as a parent, you can share moments like this with your children.* Show **COURAGEOUS** clip 11, "Adam and Dylan Run" (2:26).

Depending on your group, you may choose to share or ask someone to share how a father-figure stepped into a less-than-ideal situation to provide positive influence. Use this example as a model for what children might need from mentors.

Ironically, Derek had once been interested in Nathan's daughter and now Nathan comes to serve as a mentor to Derek, in jail. Ask the group to think of the ways they might mentor someone who is not a family member.

10-4 MEN and 10-4 WOMEN—Move into gender-specific groups if this is your practice. How might spouses decide together to open their home and hearts to kids who need godly examples?

TAKE THE WHEEL—Close by sharing some of the elements of "A Prayer for Courage." Highlight readings for the week.

SESSION 8
Surrounding Yourself with Accountability

COURAGEOUS clip 12, "Resolution Ceremony" (3:40)

➔ **All video clips are available for free at lifeway.com/courageous**

BRIEFING—Welcome the group and thank them for their participation and commitment. Start the session by giving instructions concerning a resolution ceremony or celebration event planned. Ask anyone to share a testimony of how someone in this group has impacted them over the past few weeks.

Call on someone to pray for your time together. As the group shared earlier concerning how different members made an impact on them, share that those lessons can continue: *We still have these relationships with which to encourage and inspire one another.*

In "The Week in Review," see pages 117–18 in *The Resolution for Men*, for possible answers to, "How would teaching your children to fear the Lord impact your parenting?"

STAKEOUT—Distribute Scripture references for **activity 4** to members before the session starts so they will be ready to read each one aloud: Psalm 1:1-3; Proverbs 13:20; Proverbs 27:17; 1 Corinthians 15:33; Galatians 6:1-2.

Show **COURAGEOUS** clip 12, **"Resolution Ceremony" (3:40)** and remind the group that they may be participating in something similar in the future: *The power of such an observance is in making this commitment both to each other and to God.*

10-4 MEN and 10-4 WOMEN—Think seriously about the best way to stay accountable to God and to others who support you in your goal to be a godly parent.

TAKE THE WHEEL—Encourage the group to take next steps. Announce any events planned or accountability groups scheduled. Suggest men take this step on their own if groups are not immediately available. Conclude: *Even though we are no longer meeting, there are some final readings that "tie up" what we have discussed today.*

ENDNOTES

SESSION 1
1. Mark Kelly, "Lifeway Research looks at role of faith in parenting," [online], 24 March 2009 [cited 14 July 2011]. Available from the Internet: *www.lifeway.com.*
2. A. W. Tozer, *The Knowledge of the Holy* (New York: HarperCollins, 1961), 1. Available from the Internet: *www.amazon.com*

SESSION 2
1. Adapted from *Experiencing God's Grace* (Louisville, KY: The Southern Baptist Theological Seminary, 2009). Available from the Internet: *www.sbts.edu/documents/GRACE.pdf*

SESSION 3
1. *English Standard Version Study Bible* (Wheaton, IL: Crossway Bibles, 2008), 1859.
2. Ibid.
3. "Top Ten Facts on Fatherhood," *National Center for Fathering* [online], 2010 [cited 25 July 2011]. Available from the Internet: *www.courageousresources.com/mensministry*

SESSION 4
1. "I Learned It By Watching You," *Anti-Drug PSA Commercial,* [video, cited 25 July 2011]. Available from the Internet: *www.youtube.com*

SESSION 5
1. Jane George, "Polar bear no match for fearsome mother in Ivujivik," *Nunatsiaq News* [online], 17 February 2006 [cited 26 July 2011]. Available from the Internet: *www.nunatsiaqonline.ca/ archives/60217/news/nunavut/60217_03.html*